LEADERS DON'T HAVE TO BE LONELY

ELIMINATE THE LONELINESS AND LEAD LIKE A COACH

By Robin M L Johnson, DSL

For general information on our other products and services see the authors website at www.designorgsolns.com or call (630) 936-7709.

Library of Congress Cataloging-in-Publication Data

Published by: Envise, LLC, Naperville, Illinois

Cover & Interior Design by: Jasmine Womack

Johnson, Robin M. L., 1968 –

Leaders don't have to be lonely: eliminate the loneliness and lead like a coach

Library of Congress Control Number: 2014903944

ISBN 978-0-991-50820-4

10 9 8 7 6 5 4 3 2 1

1. Leadership Loneliness 2. Coaching 3. Coaching Leadership I. Title

Second Edition

Printed in the United States of America

TABLE OF CONTENTS

PART I

LEADERSHIP LONELINESS

DEDICATION

Dedicated to my mom, who always knew I could accomplish such a lofty goal, and to Derek Stovall-Leonard, who encouraged me, and created the space to write this book.

Part I

Leadership Loneliness

INTRODUCTION

Employees don't talk to you? You can't understand why you are always the last one to find out what's happening in your department? Employees stop talking when you enter the room? There is simile between your department and a revolving door?

Leaders Don't Have to Be Lonely will help new managers understand the distinct difference between being a manager and being a leader. While managers concentrate on budgets, metrics, marketing, and customers, leaders also manage those things while developing and maintaining relationships with their employees. When managers choose not to lead, and dismiss the idea of developing relationships with their employees, they lose because they eventually experience what we call, "Leadership Loneliness."

Leadership loneliness is a phenomenon felt by many leaders both in the boardroom and on the front line. Although, many leaders think experiencing loneliness is inevitable, it can be avoided. Leaders can do something about it. In part one of the book, managers will learn the three most common reasons why they are likely to experience loneliness and isolation. They will also learn that loneliness and isolation, if it persists, can impact their mental and physical health, which can ultimately affect how they lead.

In part two, the discussion changes and managers learn how they can chart a new course to eliminate the loneliness and isolation they experience. Of course, eliminating loneliness and isolation implies something will have to be done entirely different than what was done before. The difference suggested here is in the manager becoming a coaching-leader.

Because coaching-leadership is a relationship-based leadership style, there is no possible way to discuss the matter without delving into the architect of relationships. Good working relationships are the outcome of establishing trust, and managers who work to bring life to relationships with their employees experience twofold benefits; 1) when employees feel listened to (an element of relationship building) their stress is reduced and business performance improves; and 2) the leader feels a sense of purpose and satisfaction knowing they made a difference in someone else's life.

Finally, the story would not be complete without sharing ways in which to carry out the coaching-leadership responsibility. If there is a desire to make the transformation from manager to coaching-leader, then leaders will find a coaching model and coaching forms to help get them started.

CHAPTER ONE

LEADERSHIP & LONELINESS

Manager vs. Leader

Being promoted into a management position does not make one a leader automatically. Many new managers think they are leaders, and wish to be, because of the prestige, benefits and the influence it affords them. However, what business school professors and leadership pundits fail to mention is this: as a new leader, one is in a minority group with responsibilities and pressures likely to exceed their capabilities and capacity.[1] Being a leader is far harder than it looks because not only are they responsible for all that goes into producing, marketing and selling goods, but they are also accountable for people[2] - the most challenging of all variables to manage.

Leadership is about having the ability to influence others. There is often confusion about what leadership really is because the word has become almost ubiquitous and synonymous with what usually occurs in the workplace by those in authority: management.

Management is defined by the actions of a group of people who achieve orderly results by controlling schedules, policies, procedures and budgets.[3] Yet leadership is a process grounded in relationship and is based on the ability to influence followers to create change and attain their goals.[4] It is critical in the new manager's role to understand what it takes to lead. A lack of healthy leadership will restrict organizational growth and success. Let's be clear, managers are greatly needed. They are well adept at managing budgets, policies and procedures, and can even maneuver through and manipulate office politics. But what is missing, most often, is the innovation and encouragement to change and grow, which comes with leadership skills.[5]

Managers in the educational arena are evaluated on their students' reading and math scores. Those in manufacturing management are judged on the number of cases, which can be produced by shift's end. And sales managers will be seen as a value add if they consistently make their quarterly sales number. However, regardless of their product (good scores, cases, or sales, respectively), the ability to make product successfully is predicated upon the manager's ability to influence their employees. Therefore, managers must learn how to engage an employee's knowledge, skills and abilities and find creative ways to release their energies to fulfill the organization's mission and vision.[6] Managers who can successfully accomplish this are on their way to becoming leaders, and more specifically, coaching-leaders. How the manager engages their employees' knowledge, skills and abilities will be the key to their own success, and in large part, will determine their ability to make evolutionary steps from manager to coaching-leader.[7]

Managers who wish to become leaders are responsible for those whom they lead: employees, who reinforce their decisions, assume responsibility, serve, challenge the status quo, and participate in transformations.[8] It is imperative for new managers to recognize both they, and those who follow, together play a critical role in the rise or the fall of the organization. And though they each play a different role, they complement one another, and therefore should not be in competition with each other.[9] They are each two sides of the same coin, with no means of operating an organization independent of one another.

A Leader's Influence

New managers might feel like targets with darts being hurled at them from every direction. Yet, successfully navigating their way around those darts, in order to accomplish their goals, will mean learning that the key to leadership is gaining the ability to influence not only their workforce, but also their boss and every other stakeholder to whom the organization is responsible (e.g. customers, shareholders, executive board, parents, and the community).[10]

Influence comes from the leader

- Being a good listener

- Remembering names

- Being genuinely interested in others

- Letting others talk

- Showing respect for others' opinions, and

- Admitting when they are wrong or have made a mistake[11]

These habits are essential for any manager seeking to transition into a coaching-leader function. And, in fact, the authors of Leadership Mystique argue, if a leader gets derailed, it is more likely to be caused by a lack of interpersonal skills rather than by an insufficient knowledge of the latest techniques in education, marketing, finance or production.[12] So a manager must take the responsibility to influence earnestly, as it may be the most significant part of the leadership process.[13]

Leadership Loneliness and Isolation

We started by introducing the idea that leaders are in a minority group with responsibilities and pressures that, at least in the beginning, are likely to exceed their capabilities and capacity. Unfortunately, being in the minority often leads to isolation and loneliness. Many leaders feel loneliness or isolation at some point during their tenure, as taking on the new role often means separating from friends and having to make tough decisions on their own.[14]

In speaking with a number of middle managers while researching for this book, it is noteworthy, they all said loneliness was a struggle when they were first promoted into the managerial role, especially when they found themselves managing their peers. One common reason for this loneliness is the push and pull effect, which happens when peers begin to slowly push away as they deal with their own mixed feelings of happiness, envy, abandonment or being overlooked, while at the same time the manager's new colleagues pull them into the realm of scheduling, budgeting, head counts and strategy.[15] Some new managers find this tension a bit disconcerting, as all these people make relentless, and perhaps even, conflicting demands on them.[16] They are not alone if they do. In fact, half of all CEOs report feelings of loneliness, with nearly 70% of first time CEOs experiencing this phenomenon.[17] Their level of responsibility virtually invites it. For them, there is the onus of being forced to make the tough decisions alone, without supporters, mentors, or true corporate friends, which creates a sense of loneliness few people experience.[18]

Loneliness - a sadness felt from having a lack of camaraderie, and isolation - a phenomenon felt when loneliness persists, should be seen as a warning sign that something is not right. Loneliness causes people to feel empty, alone and unwanted, and people who are lonely often crave human contact, but their state of mind makes it more difficult to form connections with other people.[19] If managers are feeling lonely and isolated, they should take it as a sign that they should take more interest in their relationships. They should make the time to reach out and interact with others, whether the interaction is of a working or personal nature.

Loneliness is a "dangerous byproduct of leadership."[20] Not only are there emotional implications, but suffering through loneliness and isolation can also lead to health issues. In their book, *Loneliness*, Cacioppo and Patrick say, an individual who experiences isolation has health issues comparable to those who have high blood pressure, lack of exercise, are obese and who smoke.[21] Likewise, if an individual experiences isolation for too long, those physical ailments can begin to accelerate the aging process.[22] Although I have yet to meet a leader who is experiencing chronic feelings of isolation, the bottom line stands. Loneliness and isolation, if not treated, can lead to an early grave.

What leads to this loneliness and isolation?

As I hope it's becoming clear, leadership can be a tempestuous position. If a manager finds him or herself in this space of loneliness and isolation, they should realize it is quite prevalent and, in some respects, unavoidable. Even the greatest of leaders have all experienced this deep sense of separation from others. Consider the lives of such biblical leaders as: David, the king of Israel, known for leading the people of Israel into victory during times of war; Paul, the converted Jew responsible for influencing Christianity by evangelizing throughout the Roman Empire; and Jesus. Or we can consider the likes of America's leaders, such as Harry Truman,[23] George W.

Bush,[24] and Martin Luther King.[25] These men each had to deal with their own bouts of loneliness and isolation, in the midst of being physically surrounded by others. They were unable to escape these feelings of isolation, and new managers are just as unlikely to escape it if they do not learn to lead differently.

These great leaders likely experienced loneliness and isolation because they were misunderstood, hated, and rejected by people who did not want what they had to offer. New leaders today, on the other hand, often feel lonely and isolated because their own behavior incites it, and determines the degree to which it is experienced. A great example of how behavior will increase one's loneliness is in Patty's story.

Patty

Patty, a newly promoted manager, was tasked with creating a new department. Prior to accepting the job, Patty was an independent contributor in the microbiology department. With no previous experience with the work required to meet the goals of the new department, she was given the role primarily because she was the only one willing to take the responsibility, which isn't uncommon.

Patty was an exemplary employee in her previous function, however as a new manager of a new department, with employees who had varying degrees of experience in the work required, she lacked the skills and character qualities needed to effectively lead. Patty's team included a mélange of professionals from diverse backgrounds. Made up of all types, from seasoned training professionals with advanced degrees to a chemist. Each team member was a subject matter expert in their respective fields, which made the dynamics of the group quite interesting. They were a small team with the potential to make a huge impact on the rest of the organization, if the right leader had been put in the role.

The staff's perception of Patty was that she stirred up strife. Not only did she not mind if there was contention between them, she often instigated it. In fact, they believed she reveled in the fact she could use their strengths and diversity to pit them one against another. As a result, the team interacted with each other gingerly and only communicated with her when it was absolutely necessary, like during staff meetings. Those staff meetings were all business with no superfluous exchange of words.

Despite her actions to keep the team at variance with one another, they would occasionally go out for lunch or sit together at company-sponsored events without inviting her to join. On occasion, someone would feel sorry for her and ask if she'd like them to bring her some lunch back, but rarely was she invited to hang out with them. Oftentimes when she'd schedule lunch to celebrate a team member's birthday, the lunch would be canceled as, one by one members of the group would find a reason to back out.

One day, while in Patty's office, she tearfully told me that she felt isolated at work. I listened and allowed her to communicate what she was feeling. It was then I realized her actions caused an awful reaction from her staff.

This raises the question: Could Patty's tenure as manager have been less painful for her? Absolutely! Did the team's actions help intensify the loneliness she felt? Of course it did! However, their actions were an effort to avoid unnecessary drama her presence created.

Leadership Training Needed

It has often been said, an organization loses a great technician and gains a poor manager - mediocre at best - when an employee with excellent technical skills is promoted into a managerial position. This case is no different. Patty lacked some much-needed leadership skills, but she also possessed technical skills quite valuable to the operation of the business. New managers are often promoted into positions of management because of their technical ability. According to a study done by the Center for Creative Leadership, at least 50% of new managers were promoted because of their technical skill.[26] However, the problem is, they are rarely trained to be leaders prior to accepting their position. This lack of leadership training further perpetuates loneliness in the workplace.

Prior to beginning a management position, one of the most significant lessons a new manager can be taught is, the manager creates the climate and culture by their values, which are defined by their personal motives, ethics and morals.[27] The climate created will determine the level of loneliness and isolation the new manager experiences by those whom they are responsible for influencing. With that said, "Loneliness and isolation are the natural destinations for managers who have not purposefully chartered another course."[28]

If managers like Patty want to chart a course away from loneliness and isolation then they must create an alternative future, which can only happen through a shift in their language, beliefs and behavior. In other words, if they want a change in their culture, the key is in changing the conversations they have.[29] This is a must if they want to intentionally influence the level of engagement between their employees and themselves.

One such way to change the conversation, and increase the influence as a leader through communication, is to adopt a coaching leadership style. Coaching-leadership fosters trust and self-reflection through the use of deep inquiry, while helping to unlock an employee's potential to maximize their own performance.[30] A manager will find that the willingness to coach in their managerial role will satisfy a leadership behavior most desired by subordinates.[31] If leaders will help employees meet their needs, employees will reciprocate, thus reducing the leader's level of loneliness.

Lastly, although there has been an effort to make it clear that a manager's behavior will affect their level of loneliness experienced, their behavior is not the only factor to be considered. As will be seen in the upcoming chapters, organizational design and structure, technology, and even employees can also influence a manager's struggle with loneliness and isolation. Understanding how each of these elements will affect managers and their attempt to change the course of loneliness in their role will aid in making them a more effective leader.

CHAPTER TWO

WHY EMPLOYEES WON'T TALK TO YOU

Employees don't Trust You

If I had a quarter for every time I've told a manager that they do not know everything that's happening within their organization, I'd have a trunk full of quarters! Likewise, I've also had just as many conversations with employees that their managers are not following up on issues because employees are not making them aware of those issues. Unfortunately, neither group is listening. Through dialogue I've had with both managers and employee groups, I've learned managers are convinced their employees share everything with them about the business, and employees are equally convinced management has been told of the issues, and just refuse to do anything about them. There certainly is a disconnection here.

After informally polling hundreds of individuals concerning their willingness to share work-related issues with their manager, those who responded said they do not share all work-related issues with their managers; some responding more emphatically than others. The responses included:

- *"Nope, don't trust her."*

- *"No way…!!!"*

"They don't want or need to know all. Especially, if you want to demonstrate your abilities, take care. Only key facts should be told so that they are informed where they need to be."

"NO WAY! He doesn't need to know everything."

"No. Only what he needs to know. ...because he's not my boss, more of a guide for my brilliance."

"I tell him only if it is work related. I would however let him know if something was happening that I think he needs to."

"I don't believe it's the role of the employee to do so. It is the role of the manager or supervisor to have a finger on the pulse on almost everything that is taking place within the department or organization."

As a follow-up question, I asked, "If you do not share everything, why not?" Unanimously, the answer was lack of relationships; lack of trust. Over and over what I heard was, managers do not take the time to build relationships; therefore, employees do not trust their managers enough to share relevant information the manager might need to make informed decisions. What I learned from the respondents seem to be consistent with the research which says, employees are likely to filter information they communicate upward when they lack trust in their supervisor.[1] A new manager's willingness and ability to build trust is essential as trust plays a major part in shaping an employee's behavior towards the manager.[2] New managers who can prove themselves trustworthy will have a much easier time creating the relationships with employees they need to be successful. The authors of "A Conceptual Model of Leadership Transition" puts it like this, if new managers can make positive impressions, including proving themselves trustworthy, quickly, they will be identified as high potential managers, enticing employees to want to develop relationships with them.[3]

Having the trust of employees is important for the attainment of important business information, but a lack of trust and relationship is just another reason why employees do not talk to managers. Looking at further research we find that organizational silence also indicates that roughly 85% of employees confront issues of underperformance, dishonesty, inefficiency, and poor management, but will not disclose this information to their managers. Many decline to do so because of fear, insecurity or a perception that there will be a lack of reception by management. And as a result, managers are left ignorant of, and are often unable to discern, what is happening within the organization.[4]

If 85% of employees are not disclosing important elements of dysfunction to the manager, then being able to complete projects will be the least of his worries. If the new manager doesn't get accurate feedback or honest advice, because employees do not feel comfortable providing them with information, the manager's decision-making ability will be severely hindered.[5] Miscommunication, or the lack thereof, will ultimately impact the manager's effectiveness to lead. According to Milliken and Morrison, an organization's senior managers may need information about what is and is not working in order to ensure the future effectiveness of their organization.[6] Managers must be knowledgeable about their departments if the bottom line is to be met.

If new managers want to know what's going on in their organizations, all they have to do is ask one of their employees. Employees usually know what's happening at front line levels of the organization because they talk to one another.[7] Therefore, neglecting to talk to employees will result in creating an employee silence milieu where employees who might otherwise speak up and openly state their views or opinions about workplace matters, such as the actions or ideas of others, or suggested or needed changes, will shut down.[8]

Teresa

A few days ago, I was talking to a friend who is a principal of an elementary school. She had just on-boarded a new assistant principal. Her conversation with this assistant principal went something like this, "Make sure you tell me everything because I want to know everything that's happening. I don't want to be surprised and learn about things while I'm sitting in the meeting with my boss." At which point I asked, "Well you know, as the principal you are never going to know everything, right?" She responded in a way I've seen many times before when I've asked this question to managers. She was a bit taken aback as if the question asked had just posed a threat to her intellect. However, she responded that she did know, and she expected her staff to go to the assistant principal because they will see him as an advocate rather than approach her, the enforcer of the rules.

Why are managers so surprised by this fact? I'm not sure, but I find that the managers I speak to are at either ends of the spectrum. Either they think their employees tell them everything, because they are "great bosses," or they are aware their employees do not tell them everything because they've already had the misfortune of learning information in passing from a colleague outside of their department, or while sitting in a meeting with their own manager.

The fact is, the lack of relationship, which comes from a lack of trust often provokes employee silence. However, fear of the manager, or the manager's response to bad news also plays a critical role in employee silence.

Silence because of fear

What employees perceive as the prevailing 'climate of opinion' is what determines an employee's willingness to express his or her own opinion.[9] Also, employees are not likely to speak up if by doing so, they might hurt someone else in the process, be labeled as a complainer or troublemaker, or might be rejected by colleagues.[10] How often have you seen employees withhold damaging information about the organization because they fear looking like a snitch before their peers? Being perceived as a team player is much more important to most employees than risking the threat of isolation, or risk being ostracized by colleagues.[11]

Employees have also learned that speaking out can be a risky proposition and have seen the unfortunate abuse shown to coworkers who dared to confront the manager with news or information contradicting what the manager wants to hear, so they remain silent.[12]

I have seen managers yell at employees because the employee mentioned an idea the manager was not ready to hear. Two stories come to mind. One afternoon, while sitting in the office of the senior leader of an organization, having a discussion with several other managers, someone around the table was making an argument as to why a certain matter should be considered when all of a sudden, the senior leader yelled out, "Stop talking!" The outburst was strange, and the senior manager left everyone in the room completely perplexed, but also fearful of saying anything else. The discomfort in the room was ever present and the meeting ended immediately. We left the office, and a few of the managers did what employees often do, discussed the incident in the hallway. Later we found out the senior manager was going through some personal issues, and the matter mentioned during the meeting reminded him of the pain he was in. Unfortunately though, his outburst had given his managers reason to be apprehensive about bringing up matters again.

The second situation includes a manager from a quality assurance department and his boss, the director of quality. The background story is, the manager and the director were colleagues at a previous company. When the director was hired, she brought in this manager to assist her in building the quality department. One day there had been an incident in the lab, which had not been corrected in a timely manner, nor documented properly. And even more importantly, the problem had not been addressed with the director, who later found out about the matter during an inspection by the Food & Drug Administration (FDA). Finding out about the incident sent the director into a fury no one in the company had ever seen before. The manager was in his office when the director stormed in, slammed the door shut and proceeded to use every curse word in the dictionary to reprimand him. Angry she had not been told of the incident and that she had to find out through the FDA inspector. She was livid, to say the least, and everyone on the floor knew it because her outburst was so loud, that even behind closed doors, everyone heard her. It was all anyone talked about for the rest of the afternoon.

I bring up the fact that the manager and director were colleagues from a previous company because it is important to note, a relationship had already been established between the two of them. At their previous company they were both managers and reported up to the same person. The subordinate was likely aware of her temperament, but he had not experienced her as a boss until now. It is unknown why he had not made her aware of the incident. Maybe he knew telling her about it would cause her to fly off the handle, which he was trying to avoid. He likely thought the problem could be worked

19

out before she found out about it. Unfortunately for him, the FDA came in for a surprise visit, which is not uncommon.

The consequence of the director's explosion was the manager's resignation, which came the following morning. But worst yet, employees throughout the organization were afraid of her and tried avoiding her at all cost.

What happens when the manager responds in this way to an employee with whom he or she does not have the same relationship; whose interaction is not frequent enough for the employee to know the manager's bark is not as bad as it seems? What happens is the employee unfortunately learns that raising issues can be a costly blow to either his ego or to his job and so, he remains silent.

Distrust and fear are reasons why employees will not share information with you directly. However, as you progress up the organizational ladder, understand that employees will talk to you even less because your direct reports, and those you surround yourself with, will eventually begin to shelter you from bad news. Only telling you what they think you want to hear.[13]

Silence because employees think it's your job to just know things

As we learned from the responses of the unofficial survey, sometimes employees just expect their managers to know what's going on in their organizations without input from their employees. One of the individuals polled stated, he thinks it is the manager or supervisor's role to have a finger on the pulse of almost everything taking place within the department or organization. When probed further to find out why he felt it was not the employee's responsibility to voluntarily divulge information to the manager, he stated, "As a manager, one has to interact with their employees through team building projects and weekly meetings if they want to know what is going on in their organization." In other words, it is up to the leader to spend time developing healthy relationships to get the information if they want it.

It's easy to see why employees might have this perception of their managers when new managers can be guilty of having a know-it-all attitude.[14] Managers who are know-it-alls communicate to their employees that they have all the answers and often reject new perspectives, suggestions and any other valuable information needed to make informed decisions.[15] Managers with a know-it-all attitude are also less likely to ask questions, listen, or otherwise encourage an open flow of information, which drives employees away.[16]

Eliza

As a result of some organizational changes, Eliza, a sanitation manager had been transferred to a department, in a new division, about which she admittedly knew very little. As part of this transition, she inherited an existing team of supervisors and hourly employees, who had already gone through a number of managers and role changes throughout the years. Eliza did not take much time getting to know her team, their duties or their capabilities before she began reassigning them to different positions. This, of course, made her team very upset. Eliza also did not refrain from throwing fellow department managers under the bus during staff meetings, when she saw an opportunity to wield her knowledge about a process, she thought they were inadequate at performing. Shortly after making her transition to this new division, Eliza found herself managing two departments, after one department manager was demoted.

Because of Eliza's own admission, her team knew she didn't know how to run the department that she had inherited, yet they were unwilling to help her because they saw her as a know-it-all, a backstabber and a person who only cared about her own success.

Charlie, one of the supervisors in the department at the time, had come to me for some coaching, seeking assistance on how to address an issue with Eliza. As Charlie and I discussed her challenges, it became clear Charlie was reluctant to share any information with Eliza. When I addressed this issue, Charlie's response was, "she knows everything else, let her figure it out on her own."

What a dangerous place to be in as a new manager. First impressions matter and showing employees you know it all means risking the ability to develop the best strategy to move the organization forward. It also means risking the opportunity to build a coalition with employees, which will eventually lead to feelings of isolation and loneliness.[17]

By nature, a coaching-leader's role will eradicate any possibility of a leader being seen as a know-it-all because coaching-leaders are open to not knowing, and therefore, they ask powerful questions; questions evoking discovery, insight, commitment and action.[18]

CHAPTER THREE

YOUR TECHNOLOGY IS MAKING YOU LONELY

Today's Technology

No truer words have ever been spoken about technology and its impact on human relations than when sociologist Philip Slater, wrote in 1970 that "One of the major goals of technology in America is to 'free' us from the necessity of relating to, submitting to, depending upon, or controlling other people."[1] This is especially true as we consider how smartphones have inundated our society, pushing out the need to develop social interactions with one another face-to-face.

If I told you the number of smartphones being globally is estimated to be 2.5 billion by 2019, you probably wouldn't even bat an eye. And the reason is because our smartphones and tablets have become commonplace in our world today. Your entire generation, those of you born after 1980, are completely unfamiliar with a life outside of these tools. If there is any contempt for all things non-digital, it is a result of being born into a media-rich networked world, where your digital lifestyle is about more than just cool gadgets, but also about engagement, creativity, and empowerment.[2]

In today's society, electronic gadgets have become an extension of our hands, and even a few moments without them can be the basis of a major meltdown. Even those of us a bit older than the digital generation (who are familiar with the days when the house phone, or a face-to-face visit was the only way to communicate with friends outside of work and school) find it difficult to stay away from our tablets and smartphones.[3] It is completely understandable the dependence we have on our technological tools. Technology has become a ubiquitous engineering, making it almost impossible to do anything without having to sign up or log in to an account. As Sherry Turkle says, "The networked life… always on and (now) always with us, we tend the Net, and the Net teaches us to need it."[4] This is an incredibly profound assertion. The more we use the net, the more we have to use the net, which is why it is of the utmost importance that as a new manager you learn how being networked and tethered to your devices can affect your effectiveness in day-to-day activities. Instead of focusing on the use of technology itself, let us turn our attention to the ability users have to interact with other people, and more specifically how technology impacts the interaction between leaders and their followers.

How often have you been in a conference room, preparing for the meeting to start, and all the attendees of the meeting were paying more attention to their phones, or tablets, than they were to each other? Perhaps they will look up just long enough to greet those entering the room, but then they quickly go right back to looking at their mobile. You may have even noticed these same people paying more attention to their gadgets than they are to the presenter during the meeting. Everywhere we go we see people who are more engaged in their smartphones and tablets than they are with other people. We meet fewer people, spend less time gathering with others, and when we do gather, our bonds are less meaningful and less easy.[5] We are living in isolation and yet we have never been more accessible.[6] In many cases, the network has replaced the space in which we once built relationships. Our networked life has become an entertainer, comforter, and friend, and occasionally as a way to avoid others, when we would rather not be bothered. Giles Sades argues, we look to machines to perform human functions, such as providing communications, calculations, care and company.[7] We are tethered to the network, at great cost. The cost being:

- The decline in human relationships

- The inability to negotiate body language

- Inept at dealing with social rejection, and an

- Inability to work through conflict resolution[8]

Essentially, the network robs leaders and their followers the integrity of being present and in the moment.

Negotiating Body Language

There is a well-known quote by Ralph Waldo Emerson, which says, "Your actions speak so loudly that I cannot hear what you say." In other words, our actions communicate far more than our words ever have. According to Glen Ebersole, body language, or nonverbal communication, is a second source of human communication after conversation, and is often more reliable or essential to understanding what a person really means and what is going on beyond the words.[9]

Albert Mehrabian is credited with the popularly known statistics on communication patterns, which says only 7% of a face-to-face spoken message is actually conveyed by words. The remaining 38% and 55% make up vocal tone and facial and body expression, respectively. However, it is interesting to note here that his research, which was conducted and published in professional journals in the late 1960s, and has since been used by professional trainers as a guide when designing and presenting instructional materials, was not substantiated for normal everyday conversation. A number of researchers and Neuro-Linguistic Programming professionals have refuted this claim as illogical because the words actually spoken are just as valuable.[10] Dr. Judith Pearson, a Licensed Professional Counselor, argues that values, meanings, emotions, attitudes and beliefs cannot be measured and quantified, so we should place equal value on all three patterns of communication.[11] So it seems this 55/38/7 percent rule has been debunked, which means taking time to converse with employees face-to-face, in order to actually hear the words, is still needed. Necessary because fully understanding the entire message requires all of the communication patterns to be taken into account. And though Dr. Pearson argues, words are just as relevant, this does not mean tone and body language are any less significant. Again, they are equally important and when employees communicate primarily through electronic networks it hinders the manager from getting critical information from and about the person with whom they are communicating. Using emails and text messages to communicate means there is an opportunity for tone and context to be misread[12] and the manager misses the chance to see or hear what employees are not saying with their words. Consider this scenario:

You have sent a message through email to an employee inquiring about an approaching deadline for a project you will need to report back to senior management. The employee sends you a response assuring you he is working feverishly to get the project completed. He gives you a bulleted update, and is not hesitant to mention that he is waiting for responses from a few colleagues in order to complete a particular part of the project. You skim over parts of the email because it is rather lengthy, and in the midst of skimming, you receive a text message from a special someone, who you then spend the next fifteen minutes texting back and forth. Before you know it, it is time for your next meeting. A week later, the day of the report out meeting to the senior management team, you learn that while the majority of the project is complete, not all of it has been. You are angry with the employee for not telling you he was having a difficult time getting things done. And you are embarrassed as you report to the management team that the work has not yet been completed.

There are several learnings we can take from this scenario. One, the onus of communicating with the employee was on the manager. He allowed his text messages to distract him from the employee's communication and failed to communicate with the employee, via a face-to-face discussion concerning the project details, prior to the meeting. Secondly, the distraction of the text messages, which led to a failure to reply to the employee, may have created in the mind of the employee that the manager neither read the communication nor cared about the project. The third lesson learned is, in the absence of face-to-face interaction the manager may have missed subtle cues the employee conveyed of discomfort, worry, or even apathy that the project may not be completed on time. The face-to-face conversation would have possibly given the manager signals something was amiss and the employee had not told him everything.

It's clear having face-to-face conversations helps in negotiating body language, but even with the face-to-face, interpreting body language can be complicated.[13] Consider this, prior to the social networking takeover, if the person you were talking to shook their head in the middle of your sentence, you would know they were doing so in response to what you were saying. Now, however, if the same person shakes their head in the middle of your statement, it could very well be in response to something they read when they briefly turned their attention to the text message, which had just come through their phone. Even though technology has compli-cated our ability to negotiate body language,[14] it is still important for new leaders to pay attention to the body language of those they interact with, as doing so can save them some embarrassment and heartache. Figures 2 and 3 illustrate some of the most common nonverbal cues:

Positive Body Language Cues

Acceptance	Confidence	Expectancy
Hand to chest Open arms and hands Touching gestures Moving closer, one to another; preening Sitting on one leg (for female)	Steepling (fingers touching like a church steeple) Hands behind back, authority position Back stiffened Hands in coat pockets with thumbs out Hands on lapels of coat	Rubbing palms Jingling money openly crossed fingers Moving closer
Cooperation, readiness, openness	Evaluation	Reassurance
Open hands Hands on hips Hands on mid-thigh while seated Sitting on edge of chair Arms spread, gripping edge of table or desk Moving closer Sprinter's position Hand-to-face gestures	Hand-to-face gestures Head tilted Stroking chin Peering over glasses Taking glasses off, and cleaning Putting eye glass ear piece in mouth Pipe smoker gestures Getting up from table and walking around	Touching Pinching flesh Chewing pen or pencil Rubbing over thumb Touching back of chair on entering room Biting finger nails Hands in pockets
Self-control		
Holding arm behind back Gripping wrists Locked ankles Clenched hands		

Figure 2 - Positive Body Language Cues. Adapted from Max Wideman's Issacons[15]

29

Negative Body Language Cues (North American Gestures)

Boredom	Defensiveness	Frustration, annoyance
Doodling	Arms crossed on chest	Short breaths
Drumming with fingers; Legs crossed	Legs over chair arms when seated	Tchsk sound
Foot kicking	Sitting in arm chair reversed	Tightly clenched hands
Head in palm of hands	Crossing legs	Wringing hands
Blank stare	Fist-like gestures Pointing index finger Karate chops	Fist-like gestures Pointing index finger Running hand through hair
	Fast eye blinking (I'm lying!)	Rubbing back of neck Kicking at ground or an imaginary object
Nervousness	**Suspicion**	**Territorial claim**
Clearing throat	Not looking at you	Feet on desk
Whew sound	Arms crossed	Feet on chair
Soft whistling	Moving away from you Silhouette body towards you	Leaning against or touching an object Placing an object in a desired space
Picking or pinching flesh	Sideways glance Feet/body pointing towards exit	Elevating oneself
Fidgeting in chair	Touching or rubbing nose	Cigar smoking
Hands cover mouth when speaking	Rubbing eyes	Leaning back with hands behind head
Not looking at the other person	Buttoning coat, drawing away	
Tugging at pants when seated		
Jingling money or keys in pocket		
Tugging at ear Perspiring or wringing of hands		

Figure 3 - Negative Body Language Cues. Adapted from Max Wideman's Issacons[16]

Sometimes the difference between the words people speak, and our understanding of what they are saying comes from their body language,[17] which is why, if a manager chooses to become a coaching-leader they must possess active listening skills. As an active listener, it is expected of the leader to not only listen to their employees concerns, goals, beliefs and values, but to also distinguish between the words, the tone of voice and the body language they use to convey those thoughts and ideas.[18] Active listening is at the core of developing relationships, and more on active listening as a coaching leader skill can be found in chapter five.

Social Rejection

Since the beginning of time, the human race has had to deal with rejection. Feminist rejected bras, men and women reject each other and parents rejected their children. It turns out rejection may be just as natural as loneliness. It certainly carries similar consequences as loneliness. Like loneliness, "social rejection can influence emotion, cognition and even physical health."[19] The emotional pain one feels when rejection is experienced is equivalent to physical pain because, oddly enough, the brain recognizes social rejection the same as a physical ailment.[20] It was mentioned earlier that the physical impact of loneliness and isolation is comparable to those with high blood pressure, or to those who do not exercise, are obese or smoke. This is only the beginning of its physical impact. In addition to the physical pain your body feels, social rejection also increases anger, sadness, depression, jealousy and anxiety.[21] DeWall and Bushman says, "Social rejection contributes to aggression and poor impulse control, while reducing performance on difficult intellectual tasks."[22] Rejection has some serious implications, both physical and mental. The question becomes, what impact will these symptoms have on a new manager's ability to lead, especially if they have not learned how to handle rejection? Will rejection cause them to push employees away or embrace them? What will it look like to successfully manage their way through rejection? Let us look at Richard, a manufacturing manager, as an example.

Richard

Richard, a seasoned manufacturing manager for a company I previously worked for, was very well liked by his employees and colleagues. Always seen as highly knowledgeable and a fair senior manager of the organization, suddenly found himself on the outside of the "inner circle" when the new regime of senior managers from corporate decided to reshape the manufacturing process, which included bringing in a new manufacturing professional as senior manufacturing manager. The person, whom they doggedly pursued, was to initially report to Richard. However, this person was being offered much more money than Richard made and was being setup to eventually become his boss. The tension, this situation created, could be cut with a knife. Though this was the epitome of rejection in the workplace, Richard continued to come to work with a smile. He continued to do his job, and do it well. Eventually he left, as did other leaders who found the new regime impossible to work with, but employees were grateful for having worked with him.

Richard had a choice to make. Either he could continue to work hard and work through the pain, or allow the emotional turmoil he felt to cause self-isolation, anger, and jealousy; with the latter being used as a justification to lash out at employees, throwing colleagues under the bus, or worse, completely disengaging from the important work needed to be done. Back then, the network was email, and if you were lucky enough, you had a phone in the infancy stages of a smartphone and were able to send and receive text messages. Therefore, Richard did not have the luxury of burying his head in his smartphone and drowning out the hurt and pain of his situation. Without having the network as a go to, Richard was forced to be present and in the moment of his situation.

When confronted with rejection on this level, it is easy to see how one's ego would be damaged. However, it was important for Richard to stay in the moment, and to engage his friends by getting his hurt feelings and frustrations off his chest. Having a support system of colleagues or friends will help you heal the wound by offering encouragement, guidance and counsel,[23] while burying your head in your smartphone or tablet will not.

Our social networks are most likely merely a mirage of companionship.[24] It is not surprising we have exaggerated our relationships when we consider Maslow's Hierarchy of Needs.

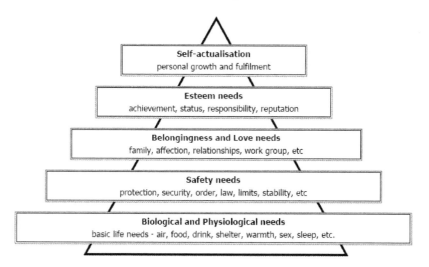

Figure 4 Maslow's Hierarchy of Needs

As Maslow's diagram illustrates, after our biological and physiological and safety needs are met we are then in need of belonging and feeling loved. The problem is our social network gives us a false sense of belonging.[25] And the countless hours spent in our social networks only numb the pain we feel, prolonging the inevitable, the need to still have to deal with the pain of rejection.[26]

I wouldn't say being inundated with social media, and technology's other uses, is the direct cause for a new leaders inability to handle rejection, especially if the leader is under the age of 35. Yet being so connected to the technology world has not helped them learn how to deal with it correctly either. As noted in the story of Richard, interacting with friends and colleagues in whom you trust is an important step to healing the ego.

When rejection is not dealt with properly, what results are antisocial behaviors and an increase in aggression.[27] Individuals oftentimes do things they later regret. Deviant actions range anywhere from annoyingly involving themselves in their employees' lives to evaluating employees more critically, and even unjustly punishing employees for even the smallest of errors.[28] The impact of this behavior results in employees who are afraid to make mistakes, which eventually chokes innovation. Antisocial behaviors and increased aggression may result in managers who make their employees feel weak, incompetent, and insignificant. And managers who behave this way will consistently underperform because this sort of treatment stifles what is needed most: fresh ideas and innovation.[29]

All over the world school shootings are becoming more and more commonplace. Look at the young men involved in school shootings in the United States in recent years. In almost every case, with the exception of cases of depression and mental illness, these were young men who felt social rejection by their peers. The rejection came in all forms, but especially in the form of bullying or rejection by girls they were interested in. And in almost all cases, these young people almost always had an online detractor.[30] It is very easy to ask the question, after the fact, why didn't this person get help? Why were his friends and family unable to recognize the signs leading to this catastrophe? But we live in a day where spending more time with our smartphone, tablet and online gaming and less in the company of real people, in real life, is typical behavior.[31] So if a young person is in deep anguish caused by social rejection, who would know it?

On a lighter note, think about the Toyota commercial of the young lady who is sitting behind her computer screen, alone, in what looks like the family room, mocking her parents because they only have nineteen friends on a social network, compared to her six hundred and eighty-seven friends. She says she is trying to convince them to become more active online because she read that older people were becoming more and more antisocial. The dichotomy of the message, as she says, "this is real living," is ironic as she sits alone and her parents are out and about living life to the fullest. This commercial is a laugh out loud funny way of selling a vehicle while exposing the reality of many of our Generation X and Millennial members. And the reality is, social rejection and the effects of it may go completely undetected because 'real living' happens behind our computer screens.

For new managers, working to overcome social rejection might be an uphill battle, but can be done through a coaching-leader style of leadership. Being a coaching-leader means being able to avoid managing through antisocial behaviors. They are able to do this by spending time being fully conscious and creating spontaneous relationships by establishing trust and intimacy with the employees.[32]

Conflict Resolution

A part of your job as a leader is to mediate and manage the conflict, which takes place from time to time.[33] Any number of things might incite a conflict, such as job performance, discrimination, rejection, or the implementation of disagreeable policies, so there's very little a leader can do to avoid them completely.[34] And no matter how unpleasant conflict might be, it doesn't have to end in broken relationships and hurt feelings, if leaders can learn how to manage them correctly. Handled well, leaders might see an increased motivation and inspiration to move forward, solve problems and enhance organizational performance.[35]

The correct handling of conflict can challenge complacency, provide the space for airing problems, foster creative and innovative problem solving, increasing the probability that the unit will respond to change and even lead to improved organizational policies and operations.[36] For these reasons, your inability, or refusal, to manage conflict can be more detrimental to the organization.

Managing conflict takes a great deal of effort, care, and thoughtfulness and will require the ability to have critical conversation. Jehn, a researcher of conflict management asserts, "conflict has the potential to provoke intense and heated discussions which are crucial for deeper and deliberate information processing, increased constructive criticism and a careful evaluation of alternatives."[37] The question is, are new managers capable of having the poignant conversations required to draw out the possibility of options among the conflicting individuals? Those conversations require face-to-face attention where they can attend to the tone, nuances and idiosyncrasies of the discussion.[38]

A dichotomy within the realm of conversation exists today. On one hand, face-to-face conversation teaches us patience because it unfolds slowly. On the other, the deluge of conversation via digital devices teaches us impatience. In our efforts to be connected and to keep the exchange going ad nauseam, we accept more people into our social networking circles with a demand for immediate positive feedback.[39] And as a way to keep the flow of exchange constant "we ask one another simpler questions; and we dumb down our communications, even on the most important matters."[40]

Face-to-face interactions are important for reasons already stated, nevertheless, it seems our communities rely less and less on them to the point that such interactions are becoming a nuisance.

Conducting a quick search on Twitter yields tweets corroborating the extreme importance of conversation via social networking sites and the desire for less face-to-face engagement. (Twitter handles have been removed for privacy).

Figure 5 Tweets taken from Tweetdeck, using search word #Conversation. Retrieved on July 20, 2013.

Within the context of belonging and of feeling accepted, conversations are to be read, not heard. Since printed conversation seems to be the more coveted choice over oral discussion, how does this affect a manager's ability to manage conflict when it arises?

Unfortunately, there is a rising and unproductive trend towards individuals trying to conduct digital conflict resolution.[41] Most likely, attempting to solve problems digitally only exacerbates the issue. Have you ever received a nasty-gram, or know someone who has, from another individual in response to a problem? Did the email resolve the problem; or rather create a bigger one? It likely promoted a reactive response sending a flurry of emails back and forth between sender and receiver, intensifying the issue while also prolonging the debate.[42] And God forbid, others were cc'ed. Now either they each have something to contribute, making matters worse, or they look on with discontent and exasperation. CC's imply the sender is either ratting out the receiver to their manager or wanting to get the cc'd involved in the conflict.[43]

Gone are the days of handling conflict behind closed doors, with all of the responsible parties in the room together hashing out their disagreement and negotiating a consensus, or compromise. Now individuals are able to express their discontent through electronic channels such as, email, text messages, Facebook, Twitter, LinkedIn and blog sites. The danger of trying to manage conflict with these measures is the absence of, or even worse, the misconstruing of emotion, tone and context, as mentioned earlier.

An attempt at squashing conflict, and the subsequent mishandling of the conflict through a social network, may cause damage to your reputation, according to reputation.com.[44] Right or wrong, how we handle ourselves on the Network is a reflection of our problem-solving and interpersonal skills, not to mention our general maturity level.[45] So as a new manager resist the urge to hide behind the Network to manage the conflict that will most certainly occur within the ranks of your department.

Renee

Renee, a young supervisor on the production floor in a large manufacturing facility, was known for being a bit rough around the edges at work, but was thought of as a sweetheart outside of the workplace and was often the center of attention when attending non work-related events. At work, however, on more than one occasion, Renee had been addressed concerning her demeanor during production meetings as she was often times slouched down in her chair with her arms folded. This demeanor sent the message that she did not want to be there. Ironically, while colleagues loved hanging out with Renee outside of work, they tried to avoid her during working hours because she did not deal with conflict very well, and would often find herself in email wars with supervisors and managers from other departments. Her fellow coworkers thought her to be a bit obnoxious when it came to dealing with her conflicts, as they could always count on Renee to manage conflict through email and include them in email rants they would rather have avoided. A number of individuals from the supervisory team approached me and ask if I could have a word with her about creating and escalating huge email wars unnecessarily. And so I did. What I learned was typical. Renee's theory was, everyone associated with the issue should have been addressed in the initial email; ignoring the fact that the issue addressed was an issue for which she primarily was responsible. Making the problem an all-inclusive one was Renee's tactic for evading any accountability for the work which had not been completed.

The goal in this chapter was to help the new manager understand how technology plays a role in their experience with loneliness. I hope it has become clear that because a lack of human interaction perpetuates even more lack of human interaction, a new manager is almost never exempt from avoiding interpersonal difficulties.[46] Therefore, social rejection and lacking the ability to manage conflict will exist. However, as a coaching-leader, the leader can learn to manage through conflict by using their active listening skills to attend to the differences in communication and goals, and then engaging in dialogue with employees concerning those differences.[47]

CHAPTER FOUR

BLAME IT ON THE CULTURE

An Individualistic culture

In general, U.S. businesses are not setup to foster collaboration between individuals within their organizations because, good or bad, North America is a culture immersed in individualism. In fact, "nothing is more American than individualism."[1] According to Marche,

> Loneliness is at the American core, a by-product of a long-standing national appetite for independence: The Pilgrims who left Europe willingly abandoned the bonds and strictures of a society that could not accept their right to be different. They did not seek out loneliness, but they accepted it as the price of their autonomy…The price of self-determination and self-reliance has often been loneliness. But Americans have always been willing to pay that price.[2]

Marche's statement may have someone asking herself, if loneliness is the price we pay for individualism and independence, then how can individuals work collaboratively, while still achieving goals, in order to reduce the loneliness leaders feel? Let's first get an understanding of what an individualistic society, more specifically, North Americans, looks like, and how this individualism affects the workplace.

In individualistic cultures, the identity and self-actualization of the person are important. Individuals think the world revolves around their values, which they also believe are prevalent around the world.[3] Americans tend to excel competitively, are achievement focused, and want to be recognized for those achievements, while at the same time they devalue the role of interpersonal relationships.[4]

This individualistic orientation is born of Anglo-Saxon men, who settled in from Europe, bringing with them their cultural values and behaviors of concern for self and immediate family.[5] Though individualism at the time had a very negative connotation than it has today, Americans have embraced the term and made it a positive.[6]

As a result of embracing this culture, America's organizations have been built on individualistic principles, and are full of individualists who are less likely to subordinate personal goals to group goals.[7] They are also likely to resist interpersonal relatedness and any social exchange, which can lead to social and emotional separation.[8]

Individualism in the workplace causes a number of challenges for both employees and the leader. One such challenge is, individualistic attitudes are less likely to create cooperative experiences, which have the ability to promote:

- greater interpersonal interactions

- greater feelings of support and acceptance by both peers and authority

- more open communication of ideas and feelings

- higher levels of trust

- greater ability to take the emotional and cognitive perspective of others,"[9] and

- are more likely to incite competition amongst its members.

Competitiveness means individualists would rather work alone to achieve their goals, though Norem-Hebeisen et al. are not sure if it's because of issues of self-confidence or anxiety about relating to others.[10]

As we discuss the culture of individualism we must not forget that individualists include new managers. Unfortunately, being a manager does not exempt you from the characteristics of individualism. Therefore, you will have to work twice as hard to develop a more cooperative attitude, or else risk falling prey to the isolation individualism causes.

Silos

As stated earlier, America's organizations have been built on individualistic principles, so does it surprise you that our companies are made up of silos (the vertical and horizontal lines in an organizational chart)? They are designed to organize the work done throughout the organization by divisions, groups and categories of people. And while organizations, to some extent, need this division to avoid disorganization,[11] these silos create predicaments of less interaction between the divisions, diminishing any knowledge sharing which could exist between groups.[12]

Figure 1 provides an illustration of how silos are created within organizations.

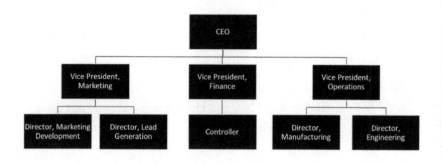

Figure 1 - Represents a siloed organization

This figure is an illustration of an organization with only one business unit. Imagine the vastness at which the organization can grow if there were several business units, with each silo creating more and more separation. The problem with silos is, the organizations, and the people in them, are both hurt by their existence.[13] Silos make it difficult to acquire information about best practices, insights and ideas. They also make it extremely difficult to share, destroys trust, cuts off communication, and fosters complacency. In addition to lack of knowledge sharing, silos also create an environment where group members, within those silos, have preconceived notions and, oftentimes, misconceptions of what the other group is doing and/ or thinking.[14]

Hierarchical structures have their advantages and disadvantages. The challenge with decentralized organizations is, each part works in isolation, occupies a world of its own and doesn't learn anything from the others."[15] It's easy to see why the decentralized structure engenders issues of loneliness and isolation. However, the beauty of decentralizing the organization is, the decentralization itself creates a smaller organization. This smaller organization becomes a cluster mimicking a collectivistic orientation, which is defined as people belonging to in-groups looking after each other in exchange for loyalty.[16] This phenomenon creates smaller pockets of individuals working together to make the smaller organization a success.

Kraft Foods

Kraft Foods, where I spent time as the Manager of Organization Development, at the time was a huge conglomerate made up of many companies and brands including Nabisco, Oscar Meyer, Cadbury, and Planters. Its many divisions were made up of biscuits and snacks, coffee, cheese and grocery, gum and candy.

In my experience, each brand operated separately, and unto itself, without the collaborative help from the other brands. Because of it, plant managers in one division did not tap into the knowledge or resources of plant managers in another division, and seldom, if ever, did the management team under the plant manager have the opportunity to interact with their counterparts throughout the other organizations. In a very stressful environment such as manufacturing, how different do you think the lives of the managers within the organization would be if they operated more as a community? How many of them felt like they were on an island left to fend for themselves? I know I often did. If I needed someone to bounce ideas off of, or was seeking advice, I often had to turn to colleagues outside of the company.

Once, at the suggestion of a colleague, I reached out to someone in another division for help with a project. This colleague had completed a similar project and was more than happy to help out. Like me, the colleague was excited to talk to someone outside of his brand, learning about what was happening in our world. He even extended an invitation for me to come see their site and how their project was moving along. I was excited to learn about other parts of the business, and to receive the help. The rollout of my project was a success, thanks in part, to him and the information he provided. Therefore, don't be afraid to reach across those siloed lines. You will benefit greatly from it.

The challenge organizations face is the possibility they will be run by a manager who is leading a group of collectivistic oriented employees, like employees from African, Asian or Latin descent. Such groups live within a collectivistic subculture and are more likely to exhibit a sense of closeness with each other and work together to accomplish their goals.[17] Within the collectivistic culture conflict is more likely to be resolved via consensus and compromise, and hierarchy is not required to impose authority since loyalty is so well internalized.[18]

Chip Starnes

Consider Chip Starnes, the U.S. CEO and President of Specialty Medical Supplies, whose company was located near Beijing. He was held captive for six days by plant employees who were demanding they be paid severance packages identical to recently laid-off co-workers. This protest came after hearing rumors that the entire plant was being closed after a division of the company began a move to India to lower production costs. While being interviewed by the Today Show, Starnes was asked if he had contacted authorities, to which he responded, yes, but "they are hands off here. They let the workers handle it themselves."[19] The police were reluctant to intervene, because this was a business dispute to be handled by the two parties.[20] How isolated do you think Starnes felt for those six days? The lesson learned here is managers can feel further isolated if your behavior contradicts the behavior of those who work for you. So do yourself a favor by observing your employees and asking yourself the following questions:

1) Which orientation do they display (individualist or collectivist)?

2) Does it contradict my own behavior?

3) If their behavior does contradict my own, how can the culture be changed so we are all working together to achieve our goals?

Becoming familiar with the organizational structure, or the method an organization employs to delineate lines of communication, policies, authority and responsibilities,[21] means being aware of how those delineations will impact employees' perspectives and cultural behaviors. Will they allow for cross-departmental collaborations and knowledge sharing, or will they keep you isolated in silos? Being aware is not enough though. It is imperative you, as the manager spend time engaging employees throughout the organization in order to minimize the effects of silos being created by organizational structures.[22]

Competition and collaboration

I hope Starne's horrifying story will convince leaders of the need to understand their organization's individualistic-collectivistic make up. But if not, maybe this can persuade them of its importance by appealing to their humanistic side, the side which wants to feel a sense of belonging and love.[23] Being a part of an individualistic society, with organizations designed the way they are, means competition, rather than collaboration and cooperation, is more often the rule than the exception. Competitive settings are depended upon environments conducive for winning, excellence, and the approval of others.[24] Consider for a moment how competition converges with the individualistic environment. Managers in organizations with an individualistic orientation suffer loneliness and isolation because there is seclusion and a 'relative lack of social reinforcement,' which reflects independence and the avoidance of others.[25] In this setting people tend to work alone to achieve their goals, though collaboration and cooperation should be the goal if engagement is to be fostered and relationships created. Collaborating and cooperating will require the team's willingness to work with one another[26] and it will take both an extraordinary amount of coordination and planning to make it happen. It will also require a relinquishing of the ego and the energy to create a synergistic environment so goals can be accomplished.[27]

Coaching-leaders can help mitigate the silo effect and foster a culture of collaboration and cooperation by building relationships through coaching employees outside of the department, which will allow greater fluidity of movement, of ideas and information, throughout the organization.[28] Coaching engagements allowing for cross-functional coaching fosters the collaboration and learning H. Fitz John Porter, a prominent industrial engineer in the early 20th century passionately wrote about. He argued, there is a great need for the collaboration between managers and workers, and the incorporation of workers' ideas into managerial direction.[29] However, before workers are comfortable sharing their ideas, and managers are willing to accept those ideas, a positive coaching relationship must first be established. The relationship is a foundational stone of the coaching engagement, and is what brings life to the coaching engagement. Because the nature of the relationship is of such high importance, we will spend more time in chapter seven discussing the anatomy of a coaching relationship.

Part II

Becoming A Coaching-Leader

CHAPTER FIVE

BECOMING A COACHING-LEADER

The art of Coaching

According to the International Coach Federation (ICF)[1], coaching is a partnering between coach and client in a thought-provoking and creative process inspiring the client to maximize their personal and professional potential. Coaches honor the client as the expert in his or her life and work and believe every client is creative, resourceful and whole. The coach's responsibility is to:

- Discover, clarify, and align with what the client wants to achieve

- Encourage client self-discovery

- Elicit client-generated solutions and strategies

- Hold the client responsible and accountable

With ICF's definition in mind, coaching in a coaching-leader relationship, becomes a focused conversation, or channeled dialogue, between the leader and the employee, for performance improvement, skill development, exploring new ideas and learning. Coaching is of a highly confidential nature in which building a trusting relationship, getting the employee to commit to change and new possibilities, and holding the employee accountable for their actions, serves to unlock the employee's potential to maximize his or her own performance.[2] As a coaching-leader, the leader becomes the conduit between where the employee starts and ends in their growth process.

Coaching is similar to, but not synonymous with, mentoring, instructing, or advising. Coaching-leaders are not responsible to mentor or instruct, but to unlock an employee's potential to learn on their own.[3] John Whitmore, author of "Coaching for Performance," argues, it does not matter what it's called, as long as it is done well, and suggest its effectiveness will depend largely on the manager's beliefs about human potential.[4] Though the manager's beliefs about human potential are extremely important to the coaching process, because it is those beliefs that will affect the quality of the relationships built, it is still important to note there are, indeed, distinctions between the disciplines.

One other such distinction is, coaching-leaders engage in forward-focused conversations that are facilitated by the power of exploration. Through this process of traveling in or through an unfamiliar area with an employee, in order to learn about it, coaching creates an opportunity to "take good people and make them the best they can be, positioning them to work more effectively and cohesively in their environments, and making the most of their capabilities."[5] Asking powerful questions is key to drawing those deep things, such as passion, purpose, and desires out of a man's heart. This Socratic method of questioning helps employees become aware of their lives and impels them to seek and find answers for themselves they ordinarily would not seek. In the process, the coaching-leader gets an opportunity to employ the power of listening, which is significant to the progression. Listening is the beginning of understanding and is an extremely powerful tool. When employees feel "listened to" and understood, their stress levels fall.[6] A coaching-leader's responsibility is to learn to frame questions effectively and to listen intently, as doing so will empower employees to think more deeply about their performance and goals, and discover their own answers.[7]

Unlike other management styles, coaching is a slower process, which will require the coaching-leader to slow down and not jump from one deadline or project to another, even though they may exist in this type of environment. It requires dialogue, not just one directional interaction, but rather true discourse where nothing is assumed, feedback is shared, questions are asked, and really listening to answers occurs.[8] Basically, coaching requires heart. It requires the heart of a leader who genuinely cares about shifting the business paradigm. It constitutes an innovative management practice directly encouraging a structure for personal change and growth, for both the coaching-leader and employee, while indirectly fostering the economic and sustainable growth of the organizations the coachees represent.[9]

Coaching-Leaders

The typical business environment says managers are in control, managers know best and managers have all the answers, but the heart of the coaching-leader believes their responsibility is to let go of the command and control attitude and build experiences for employees to grow and develop professionally and personally.[10] The coaching-leader believes individuals are responsible beings who can carry out the tasks they were hired to perform; employees can make choices and risk failure because it is the risk and responsibility which will produce long-term growth in the individual;[11] and the individual knows better than anyone the purpose and passion that lies within their own hearts. A coaching-leader cannot give purpose and passion to an individual, but can only draw it out of the employee.

This empowering attitude is important for the leader who wants to be a coaching-leader, because as Whitmore stated, the coaching-leader's beliefs about human potential is important, but the leader must also possess tangible skills in order to fulfill the responsibility as a coaching-leader.

These competencies include:

Establish trust and intimacy with the employee – through a genuine concern for the employee's work performance and future career opportunities the coaching-leader, having the ability to build a bond of trust between themselves and the employee

Listen Actively – having the ability to give undivided attention while having focused conversations with the employee. Hearing not only what the employee is saying, but also what the employee isn't saying. And allowing the employee to share their thoughts, ideas and heart without judgment

Ask Powerful Questions – asking questions causing reflection, raise awareness, insight and commitment to action[12]

Communicate Directly – Be open and honest with the employee. Reframe statements and use metaphors to draw out alternative perspectives

Create Awareness – ask the right questions to evoke internal and external drivers creating a need for change, new or different ideas and solutions

Design Actions – create actions facilitating learning, accomplish agreed upon goals

Plan and Set Goals – create goals that are specific, measurable, and achievable and help employee identify and access different resources of learning[13]

Manage Progress and Accountability – Follow-up on the employee's progress and hold the employee accountable for completed actions

The leader is still responsible for managing budgets, metrics, controlling purchases and implementing the division's strategic plans but the key is, accomplishing organizational goals by creating learning opportunities for employees through coaching engagements. With these competencies in mind, I've created the following table to demonstrate what a coaching-leader's role might look like:

Managerial/Supervisory with Coaching-Leader Competencies

Integrity:	Demonstrates respect for people and the company. Maintains a respectful, diverse and inclusive work environment where decisions and transactions are transparent and objective; be discrete with proprietary information that may reduce competitive advantage and devalue creative work; hold self, employees, and the organization accountable for their actions; maintain high standards of fiscal, social, and personal trust.
Strategic Thinking: Analysis and Ideas	Reflects on the strategic direction of the department and design actions based on new learnings from learning opportunities with staff; create plans based on analysis of issues and trends, and link them to the responsibilities, capabilities, and potential of your staff.
Coaching	Engages people, organizations, and partners in developing goals, designing actions, executing plans, and delivering results; inspire trust; be open and inclusive; build relationships; tell it like it is; create awareness; discuss more; ask more questions; hold employees accountable; deliver.

Self Management	Cultivate self-awareness; recognize and own how your emotional reactions impact work performance and relationships; display honesty and integrity in relationships consistently; adapt to changes; have an ability to delay gratification; serve others by suspending one's own agenda to contribute to another; listen; communicate with a diverse group of people; manage conflict.
Continuous Learning and Development	Address gaps in own knowledge and skills; enhance coaching skills; use learnings from coaching discussions to enhance organizational learning; establish processes to promote learning
Management Excellence: Action Management, People Management, Financial Management	Accomplishes company goals by accepting ownership for accomplishing new and different requests; maximize organizational effectiveness and sustainability through coaching; ensuring people have the support and tools they need to meet current and longer-term organizational objectives; aligning productivity and quality goals with organizational goals; communicating daily on goals and operational expectations.
Resource Management: Budget Management and Management of other Resources	Creates yearly spending plan for all budget accounts; keeps appropriate records of organizational spending and tracks it against spending plan; reallocates resources as organizational change occurs; controls purchases and inventory by meeting with account manager; negotiating prices and contracts; developing preferred supplier lists; reviewing and evaluating usage reports; analyzing variances; taking corrective actions.

Figure 6 Coaching-Leader Competencies

What Coaching is Not

Just a quick word about what coaching is not. Coaching is not a platform to discipline unproductive employees who are on their way out of the organization. The worst thing an organization can do for its employees, and the coaching discipline, is to use coaching as a way to dwell on performance issues and punish employees. Focusing on performance issues puts the emphasis on trying to fix the past by focusing on any mistakes, missed deadlines, and shortcomings the employee has already had. The beauty of coaching is it allows everyone a fresh start because it focuses on what is to come. It is about taking good people and making them the best they can be, positioning them to work more effectively and cohesively in their environments, by focusing on efficiency, effectiveness, and impact. Essentially, coaching is about making the most of an employee's capabilities.[14]

Why You should want to Coach

A part of the transformation from manager to leader will require an understanding that as a general rule, employees desire their managers to behave more like coaches (asking powerful questions, listening actively, and planning/setting goals). Unfortunately, however, it is probably the least practiced leadership skill set which exists.[15] Not all employees are the same, and not every employee wants to be treated the same way, but most employees can appreciate a leader who coaches. Besides coaching being the new leadership tool in the box, let's look at some additional reasons why you should want to coach.

Leaders who coach create an environment where employees feel helped, which ultimately enhances their effectiveness.[16] Employees want to know their manager/leader is working with them, not against them. Employees want to be led but not pushed or forced, and talented employees want leaders who can expose them to new opportunities and challenges that will make them better.[17] While yesterday's employees were told to check their brains at the door, today's employees want to be empowered to make decisions and try new things. In a recent study to find out if employees wanted to be empowered the research found

All of the participants were able to describe how being able to make decisions in relation to their own work helps them to feel that they have some autonomy in their work and this can produce a sense of control, an indicator of empowerment, which is appreciated.[18]

Employees want the knowledge and skills they bring to the table to be acknowledged and respected. Frederick Herzberg, a behavioral scientist, who conducted studies of motivational influences, learned that recognition is the second strongest motivator for employees and managers who use this behavior actually motivate employees to higher levels of productivity.[19] Therefore,coaching-leaders can trust that their employees are interested in doing their jobs well. If their decisions result in a costly mistake, influence by the coaching-leader can ensure it becomes a teachable moment, even in the midst of dire consequences.

Another motivation to becoming a coaching-leader is,talented employees are seeking a dynamic and stimulating workplace where managers will engage both the employee's heart and mind by using all of their talents to contribute to high performance results.[20] Leaders who engage employees in this manner not only create a culture where employees feel appreciated, respected and valued, but also the organization experiences success from having leaders who care enough to lead with their hearts and minds.

Consider other living organisms such as plants. The more care and attention are shown to them, the more likely they are to thrive. People are no different. There is a significant amount of empirical evidence,which suggests, organizations with managers who are effective at coaching their direct reports achieve superior business results.[21]

Think about it, as managers begin coaching, there is a "not-so-subtle shift" which begins to occur in their leadership styles.[22] As a coach, the manager will begin to shift from yesterday's top-down authoritative control style of leadership to today's more expected transformational leadership style; a leadership style in which leaders lead from the heart. The benefit to this transformation is, when employees know their manager cares about them and their success, they begin to care about the success of the business.

Lastly, being a coaching-leader is not only about making employees feel appreciated and respected. The leader should feel the same respect and appreciation. You've heard it said, "It's better to give than to receive." Well, consider for a moment what a coaching- leader does for an employee. They give employees hope for a better workplace. They give employees someone who takes the time to listen. They give employees an opportunity to learn, which will eventually open the door for career and personal growth. That's a lot of giving. Giving also creates such a level of thanksgiving in the lives of those touched the giver feels better than the individual who received the attention. Giving is such a powerful gesture the writer of Hebrews says, the one who is able to give is greater than the one who receives (Hebrews 7:7).

Therefore, leaders should want to coach because they deserve to feel satisfied and purpose-filled with their job as well. Reducing loneliness in leadership is about two things: how one leads and how they feel about what they do.

CHAPTER SIX

COACHING MODEL

Setting the Foundation

We can't take for granted that transitioning into the role of a coaching-leader is going to be easy, especially if,

- The employee is cynical about the leadership of the organization,

- You are unsure what employees think of you, your motives, and your competence

- You've had significant conflicts with employees, or

- You don't trust the employee's intentions.[1]

So forging a relationship with the employee you choose to coach will be of the utmost importance.

The coaching-leader may want to start with determining if the employee is even coachable. The coaching-leader may learn the employee is indeed not ready to be coached for two very different reasons. The first being, while employees may have a desire to be coached, they may not be ready for coaching. According to Swift, author of "Are You A Coachable Team Player?" individuals may think they are, until the coach says something they disagree with or doesn't match their beliefs, and then they shut down and become disinterested.[2] The second type of uncoachable employee is the employee who needs coaching the most but may be the least motivated to participate in it. This employee, if made to participate, may not work to reach the goals which have been set, and may jeopardize the building of a coaching culture.[3] Therefore, when establishing the coaching culture, first start with employees who are ready and motivated to be coached.

Once coachable employees have been identified, the leader may choose to take an informal and spontaneous approach to forging this coaching relationship, which according to Hunt and Weintraub, is the route most often taken by leaders who coach. On the other hand, the leader may submit to a more formal process, which is typical for an expert, or external coach.[4] The formal approach prescribed to coaching includes a written or verbal agreement and is a great way for a leader to begin building the coaching relationship. This approach gives the coaching-leader an opportunity to set the foundation by explaining and making explicit their commitment to abide by the ethical guidelines (find ICF's Code of Ethics listed in Appendix B) and establishing the coaching agreement are the first steps in the formal process.[5]

If the leader chooses the formal process,it's important they first ensure the employee knows and fully understands the nature of, and the terms and conditions of the coaching agreement, including guidelines, session frequency and cost, if chargebacks will occur. The coaching-leader should be open about the methods they use, and be ready to supply the employee with information about the coaching processes involved.[6]

According to the International Coaching Federation, the coach should ensure an agreement about what is appropriate in the relationship, what is being offered, and about the responsibilities of both the employee and coach is made at the onset of the coaching engagement.[7] If the manager is coaching for improved performance, the manager must take this time to get agreement with the employee that a problem exists.[8]

Lastly, there is a huge difference in the coaching agreement when the coach is also the manager. Whereas the coaching agreement between an external coach and coachee can be terminated, at any time, if the coaching arrangement is not an effective match between the coach and coachee, the employee-manager relationship doesn't have the same luxury. An employee cannot ask for a new manager. Therefore, when the coach is the manager, a higher level of trust, communication and patience is required. The employee not only comes into the agreement with his or her desired goals, but they must also rely on their manager for work assignments, quality of working life, and the evaluation of his or her work.[9]

A Continuum of Learning

Coaching should be a continuum of learning. According to ASC-D(formerly the Association for Supervision and Curriculum Development), coaching should provide a continuum of learning opportunities to support the acquisition and use of specific knowledge, skills, and strategies.[10] Coaching provides a steady flow of learning activities from inquiry to inquiry. The continuous cycle of learning not only creates a platform for new ideas,but should also be a breeding ground for organizational learning and transformation, thereby creating a high performance, feedback rich environment.[11] This continuum should provide employees with the opportunity to address problems, gain clarity, optimize performance and learn new skills.[12] At the same time, the organization, through the coaching-leader, learns more about the problems,which exist and may be resolved.

Finding existing coaching models partial,providing benefits to the coachee only, I have created a model I believe creates abenefit for all parties involved in the coaching conversation: the employee, the organization, and the coaching-leader.

The coaching-leader model consists of five elements: 1) asking right questions, 2) reflection, 3) action, 4) learning and 5) goal accomplishment.

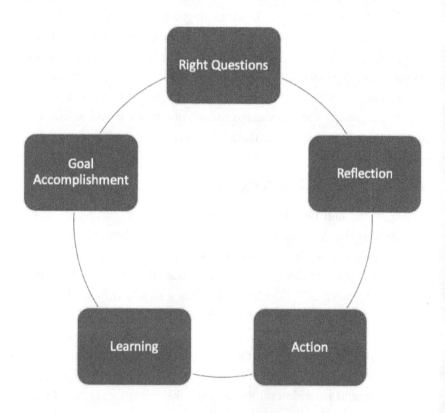

Figure 7 Coaching-leader Model

Asking The Right Questions

If having a focused conversation, fostering exploration, pushing the employee to dig deeper and reach higher, and ensuring commitment is the destination, then asking the right questions is the vehicle which gets you there.[13] Questions are the heart of coaching. Questions are what constitute "conversation" for the coach and are the beginning point for individual and organizational learning.[14] Many coaches ask questions intuitively and do not have a systematic way of thinking about, designing, asking or responding to questions.[15] However, successful coaches understand an effective coaching conversation starts with the right questions because asking the right questions, at the right time will lead to reflection. Asking the right questions is just as much about how you ask the question than what you ask. According to Whitmore, telling or asking closed-ended questions removes the onus of thinking from the coachee. Instead, the coach should ask open-ended questions as they cause the coachee to think for themselves.[16]

Asking the right question is so powerful because questions, the ones we ask ourselves, and the ones we ask to others, help draw our attention to the internal questions we have. We are often unaware of the questions residing within us even though they perpetuate our limiting beliefs,[17] which in turn drive our decisions and actions, or our lack thereof. Susan Scott, author of Fierce Conversation says it this way, "Interrogating reality, through questions, allows us to generate an internal commitment to a decision."[18] The internal commitment comes after a period of reflection, which requires a deep connection with the inner self.

The following are characteristics of right, or powerful questions:

- Questions taking the employee to a place they had not previously considered, or had not wanted to consider.

- Questions taking the employee by surprise.

- Questions probing the inner feelings and views of the employee.[19]

Reflection

A few times, when asked what I was doing, I responded with, "I am thinking about thinking about what I'm thinking about." This in essence is meta-reflection. It's going deeper to think about what you think about. It is not stopping at the first thought providing a solution. But rather, reflection is looking at our experiences and thinking about how our experiences are impacting our lives at work or personally.[20] And when done in relationship with the coach, allows the employee to go beyond their go to solutions, to add to or alter their assumptions of experiences.[21]

Reflection happens when the questions coaching-leaders ask leads to additional questions employees then ask themselves about what they really believe. In turn, dialogue is had between the coaching-leader and the employee about those views.

One cannot make a commitment to a decision and act without first taking time for reflection. Reflection goes beyond a simple act of the thinking. As mentioned in the previous section, reflection is a result of interrogating reality. In coaching, it illuminates the most fundamental assumptions about what employees have experienced, why they have experienced it, and the beliefs they have which keeps them stuck in a situation.[22] Reflecting, in this way provides a basis for future actions because it's not until the employee sees why they do things the way they do, that they can begin to make different choices going forward.

Why is reflection needed?

Reflection, by the employee being coached, has to occur within the coaching discussion because otherwise, employees "stay trapped in unexamined judgments, interpretations, assumptions and expectations."[23] These unexamined judgments, interpretations, assumptions and expectations impact employees' performance because;

1) It shuts down any chance for new ideas, data or information helping them learn from their actions.

2) They are unaware of how their limiting beliefs affect their behavior and the consequences following.

3) It creates a gap between their espoused theory and their theories-in-use. Or in other words, a gap will exist between what they say they are going to do and what they actually do. And,

4) When similar situations seem to reoccur, the employee usually looks no further than the solution they used before, in lieu of examining how the situation may be different and how a different solution may be needed.[24]

The goal is to get employees to reflect on why, what, and how they think about their circumstances and experiences. It is to tear down their assumptions in order to take action or take actions differently. Therefore, we must ask the right questions, causing an awareness of limiting beliefs to ensue. This in turn makes them more receptive to considering alternative ways of reasoning and behaving.

Prompting the Employee to Reflect

The right questions have been asked and an awareness has been raised, and the employee responds with, "Wow, that's a great question." Now the coaching-leader must help the employee get to a place where they can think deeply about where they are, where they want or need to be, and any alternative solutions getting them there. Some level of prompting will be needed to move them to this new mental model. Below is a guide a coaching-leader can use to create dialogue.

Dialogue Guide

Describing
Recognize and describe the situation or experience without assigning any meaning or evaluating the experience. Tell the employee they are not allowed to defend their reasons for acting in such a way. They are only describing the situation.
Exposing
Ask the employee to share their feelings about the experience or situation. What do they think about the experience? Why did they perform a particular action? What doubts do they have? This will cause any uncertainties and unfounded assumptions the might have, to surface.
Probing
If the employee is having difficulties explaining why they behaved the way they did, you may want to further probe and ask questions about causes, assumptions, inferences and possible outcomes.

Figure 8 Dialogue Guide adapted from Raelin's Skills of Reflective Practice[25]

Difficulties in getting employees to reflect

Unfortunately, there is hardly ever any time given for reflection. The world today does not allow time for thought, and very few senior managers will misunderstand a coaching-leader's efforts to ask questions instead of just giving instructions. Reflection and contemplation is perceived as stagnant and unproductive.[26] Our society is all about action and getting things done. Answers are wanted NOW. Decisions should be made almost immediately and any slight indication of delay is seen as a sign of weakness. Even if the delay may subsequently produce a better decision.[27]

Nevertheless, reflection is a necessity if our organizations, and the people in them, are going to grow. Reflection requires us to assess and reassess our assumptions.[28] Through reflection, learning often occurs when we realize the assumptions we have made throughout the years are found to be invalid or inauthentic.[29]

Given the scant amount of time used for reflection, most employees probably have very little practice at it. Therefore, do not expect reflection to happen instantly. A number of coaching discussions will probably be needed before the coaching-leader can get to the heart of their assumptions, and unexamined judgments. "Behavioral change takes time, and regular practice and reinforcement are critical to altering long-ingrained behavioral patterns."[30] Remember the, "Wow, that's a great question" comment? This comment may cost the coaching-leader and employee a few days of dialogue before getting a thoughtful answer. Because, truthfully, it may be the first time the employee has ever been asked the question and it may take some time to ponder it.

Also, reflection can be painful, discomforting and embarrassing even.[31] Sharing with a coaching-leader might risk damaging their self-image or self-esteem. Consequently, how much the employee is willing to be candid about the pain will depend a great deal on the level of trust which has been established between the two.

Action

Action is the next step in the coaching model I am presenting. Before the employee can take action, they must first have a desire to act on the new ideas and alternative solutions discussed during re-flection. This desire to act characterizes the motivation and ultimate choice they have in participating in accomplishing their goals,[32] and merely being aware that change is necessary is not enough to create desire.

Even when an employee initiates a conversation about needing to change, there may still be a resistance to do so. Reasons such as:

- The change may still be unclear.

- The change means having to change relationships with colleagues

- The employee is unsure about how to make the change

- The employee perceives the cost of the change outweighing the gains

- The employee thinks the change will threaten their job or their authority in an organization.[33]

Nevertheless, if the coaching-leader meets with resistance, they should ask more questions, and listen to those responses, because asking questions will help the employee rethink their assumptions, which may lead to lowered resistance.[34] What are the consequences of not taking action? What's going on in their personal life which may be keeping them from acting? What would motivate them to act? Meeting with resistance can be frustrating. This, however, is a great opportunity for the coaching-leader to learn more about their employee, which further develops the relationship. In an interview with the Harvard Business Review, Xavier Amador said managers should use the shutup, listen and win method.[35] Though shut up seems a bit rude, it gets the managers attention so he can stop dismantling and start using his authority to build stronger relationships. "That's the prize, a strong relationship."[36] A strong relationship implies less loneliness, which was the point of writing this book. If leaders lead in a coach-leadership style, loneliness felt because of a lack of interaction with employees will no longer be a factor because the interaction between the employee and coaching-leader will create an environment where relationships are forged and where learning and knowledge sharing can flourish.[37] The coaching-leader must ask more questions, intentionally listening for feedback, and resist the urge to be a know-it-all. Behaving in this manner will endear employees to you and lower any resistance they might have.[38]

Resistance may occur because of adverse reactions to the direction of the change, how the change is being handled, or merely just from people's natural reaction to change.[39] Learning why the resistance is occurring will help the coaching-leader learn of any systemic issues,which may exist within the organization. As an example, the coaching-leader may discover the employee resists because past experiences, and the culture of the organization, have taught them that doing things differently will not make a difference to the organization. They may also learn that doing things differently will upset people. This is precisely why the coaching discussion is needed and judgments should be suspended. Resistance is a resource and should be viewed as feedback.[40] So coaching-leaders should take resistance in stride. Yes, it delays progress, but from a coaching-leader's perspective, resistance does not have to be a bad thing.

Finally, the resistance is gone and the employee has a desire to act. The next step in the coaching discussion is to persuade the employee to commit to building an action plan. This means narrowing down the alternative solutions to a few,which will meet the goals identified as being relevant and needing to be accomplished. Employees may have some difficulty in selecting alternatives but the coaching-leader should resist the urge to step back into manager mode and interfere with the selection by commanding, demanding or persuading with overt or covert threats.[41] Instead, the coaching-leader can help by coaching the employee to map out the alternatives with the benefits and costs of each course of action.[42]

It is necessary for the coaching-leader to allow the employee to take ownership of the actions they are committing to. Otherwise, if the coaching-leader imposes in any way on the rights of, or desires of the employee, he may hinder the growth of the employee.[43] The coaching-leader's interference absolves the employee of any feeling of responsibility to direct his or her personal development, and this posture may result in stagnation or failure.[44] By interfering, the coaching-leader gives the employee a reason to say, "I knew it wouldn't work." Instead, the coaching-leader should continue to ask questions compelling the employee to take ownership of their actions. The coaching-leader might try the following:

- What are you going to do?

- When are you going to do it?

- How will this action meet your goal?

- What obstacles might you meet along the way?

- Who needs to know?

- What support do you need?

- How and when are you going to get the support?[45]

- What are you resisting?

- What will you gain by accomplishing this?

- What is your desire/goal?

- What are you unwilling to risk?

- What is this _____ costing you?

Action is the sole purpose for coaching.[46] Without action, all the coaching-leader has is a friendship with an employee, or just a slot of time blocked off for an enthralling conversation. Getting the employee to do something (and eradicating loneliness) should be the coaching-leaders priority, and here's why; 1) the employee will not know if the ideas generated during reflection will work if they are not acted on;[47] 2) it builds confidence where the employee lacks it;[48] and 3) action promotes learning, for the employee, the coaching-leader and the organization. All three of these priorities are pivotal for building the organization. Which leads us to the next coaching discussion.

Learning

Learning only becomes possible when someone both recognizes the need for change and sees the effects of their actions in working on a real problem. We learn best with and from other people, when addressing together pressing problems to which no one knows the solution. Learning is always for a purpose – resolving a problem or living in a more satisfying way.[49]

Learning does not happen in isolation. There must be collaborative engagement, which the coaching-leader provides with feedback and follow-up.[50] An individual can read, study, and construct new ideas but without feedback cannot know if the newly acquired ideas have been misconstrued.[51] It is not until discussion and debate are had with others that the new information can be cultivated and understood. Learning does not stop there nonetheless.

Take action and learning will occur.[52] As employees initiate action, they collect new information along the way, such as; who do they need to talk to? What do they need to know? Do they have the necessary skills to complete the task? And, if no, where do you go to get those skills? Once they acquire the answers to these questions the employee can use this information to perform their tasks. The coaching-leader in turn provides performance feedback, which will be greatly appreciated by the employee, especially if the feedback is positive, as positive feedback increases their motivation to keep moving forward.[53]

We all seek fresh input, even as small children we look for feedback. Think of a child who is being taught how to roller-skate by her dad. Initially, dad holds the child's hand as she teeters and wobbles around the rink. Every now and then, her ankles twist, she stumbles off balance and dad catches her before she falls to the floor. Occasionally, she does fall and dad is there to pick her up and encourages her to try again. After awhile the child gets the hang of it and she feels a little more confident about being on the skates. Dad then lets her go and she wobbles around the rink on her own. He remains close behind. Every few steps, she turns to dad to see if he is still nearby and calls out to him, "Dad, do you see me?" or "Dad, am I doing it?" She is looking for input, and maybe even a little validation that she is doing it right. This child is not unlike adults in the workplace. Like the dad's feedback, a coaching-leader's input will expand the employee's thought process and the knowledge base on which they can make decisions.

Many people start things, very few ever finish. Follow-up is a part of finishing and the lack of it is one of the most common reasons why employees are able to get away with unsatisfactory performance for such long periods of time.[54] Follow-up often goes neglected but does not take much time. Follow-up only requires the coaching-leader to ask the employee where they are at in completing the actions they committed to working on.[55] During the follow-up is also the time when the coaching-leader should acknowledge the employee for what they have completed, have not completed, or what they have learned or become aware of since the last conversation.[56] Maybe managers do not follow-up because they do not want to deal with the consequences of an employee who has not kept their commitments. Follow-up is crucial though, for both the employee and the coaching-leader, but particularly for the coaching-leader who should use this conversation as a learning opportunity for him or herself.

You benefit from the learning discussion too

Learning is as much for the coaching-leader as it is for the employee. Obviously, the more the employee acts on their commitments, the more learning will materialize in their lives, but the coaching discourse benefits the coaching-leader as well. Remember back in chapter four, I wrote that employees do not to talk to managers. Well, a coaching relationship creates the potential for informal conversations and spontaneous conversations to take place. As a result of these conversations, both the employee and the coaching manager learn about the problems existing within the organization and they work together to address those challenges.[57]

Goal Accomplishment

The coaching discussions have pushed employees to completing some all-important goals. In the process they've learned a new skill, obtained new information about the coaching-leader and the organization, gained a new level of confidence, and they are well on their way to meeting the next goal. Now it's time for the coaching-leader to recognize their successes. Managing progress and accountability by identifying and targeting early successes important to the employee, and celebrating those successes, is a critical part of the coaching relationship.[58] It's an important step because recognition reinforces the employee's achievements.[59] According to an International Coaching Federation pamphlet, employees have attributed coaching to the following improvements:

- 50% work performance

- 57% improvement in time management,

- 80% in self-confidence, and

- 73% in improved relationships[60]

Coaching works, and employees who have achieved goals and gained new skill sets through coaching, want to be recognized for their accomplishments. Recognition can take place at the time of achievement, or on a contingency basis; contingency recognition being a pre-arranged positive consequence to the employee's completion of his or her goals.[61] How the coaching-leader recognizes the employee's effort is up to them. Depending on the size of the goal and the effort it took to accomplish it, it may be an acknowledgement during a staff meeting or it may be a bonus check. The point is, the coaching-leader must make sure the accomplishment of the goal is acknowledged in some way.

CHAPTER SEVEN

IT ALL STARTS WITH RELATIONSHIP

Leader transitions and relationship

Building relationships is the response to loneliness and isolation. Becoming a coaching-leader will facilitate the building of those relationships. Remember, new managers, who are transitioning from one role into a manager role within the organization, are in a precarious space because they have not yet bonded with new colleagues. And friendships, prior to the promotion, have become awkward and perhaps, a little strained. It is believed managers will have to learn how to have cordial boss-employee relationships with those who were once peers. And adjusting to the new social dynamic can be one of the toughest parts of the job.[1] But coaching-leaders are impervious to this nuisance because they use the relationships with the old peer group to their advantage. The coaching-leader can also use these established relationships to build a coaching culture, one where his old peers experience a higher level of trust and openness to the management team, and where learning and knowledge-sharing becomes increasingly obtainable.[2] This also benefits the business a great deal because, when the new leader leads by coaching, they are able to transition with minimal disruption, and the organization's performance is left intact.[3]

On the other hand, a new leader to the organization will have to move deliberately if they hope to build relationships with their employees and avoid loneliness. It's during this time leaders are under intense scrutiny and have the least amount of influence on their employee's perceptions.[4] Employees are watching every move and are trying to figure out if they are going to like the new leader or hate him. First impressions are powerful, and the new leader's actions will either motivate employees to become loyal team players, compel them to fall back into the shadows, or even worse yet, turn against the new leader all together.[5] In either case, whether as a new leader transitioning from a previous role, or as a new leader to the organization, the leader will need to build healthy relationships with their employees if they want to avoid loneliness.

Transactional Leadership

Earlier in my research I spoke with a number of managers from various industries about their experience with loneliness. One new manager in particular stands out because she was aware that many of her staff members did not yet trust her as their manager, and consequently, do not share information with her. She said she often learns of information while in meetings with her boss and/or with other colleagues. And though she is aware of this, she has not done much to change their perception of her, and therefore their willingness to share with her. She, like many managers, keeps to the status quo and does what she has seen other managers do: makes the manager-employee relationship very transactional.

But the relationship cannot be transactional if the leader is to avoid or overcome loneliness. Transactional leadership works counter to building healthy relationships because as the name implies, it's a transaction between two people and not a relationship. Transactional leadership is a "cost-benefit or economic exchange" in the form of a transaction to either reward employees for achieving their expected results, or deliver a reprimand or some other form of punishment because of a lack of performance.[6] Employees know if they achieve their goals, they will be rewarded, and if they do not, they can expect to be punished. The transactional leader does not individualize employee needs or bother to focus on their personal development. A transactional leader is concerned with self and how they can get ahead.[7]

Leaders who are transactional might find themselves interacting with employees in three ways: by management-by-exception, laissez-faire or with contingent reward.

Management-by-Exception Leadership

Those who lead by management-by-exception manage by giving employees "corrective criticism, negative feedback and negative rein-forcement."[8] These leaders do not inspire employees to be extraordinary, or to achieve more than expected. As a matter of fact, these types of transactional leaders oftentimes do not address employees until, and unless, the employee is underperforming.[9] An example of this kind of leadership is a manager in customer service or a sales manager. In this case, the leader listens in on the call for mistakes and the moment the customer service rep hangs up the phone, the leader takes corrective action.

Laissez-Faire Leadership

Another type of transactional leader is one who leads in a lais-sez-faire style. This leader is lazy, non-committal, complacent, and is out of touch with his employees. Unlike a coaching-leader, a lais-sez-faire leader works hard to avoid any involvement and personal interaction with his employees.[10] This particular type of leadership is not really leadership at all. Employees with laissez-faire leaders may see very little of them because they do not have meetings, stays behind closed doors, or are otherwise unseen.

Contingent Reward Leadership

Contingent reward leadership is the third transactional leadership style. Managers who lead in this manner typically meet business needs by employing the carrot dangling from a stick method, a metaphor characterizing the use of a reward to motivate employees to perform.[11] Negotiation between leader and employee is the key to this mode of leadership. In this case, the leader works to obtain agreement from the employee on the work needing to be accomplished and the payoff that will occur when the job is complete.[12] Boxers, recording artists, actors and actresses often have managers who lead this way.

Table 1 Leadership Style Comparison

	Coaching-Leadership	Management-by-Exception	Laissez-Faire	Contingency Reward
Characteristics	Establishes trust and intimacy with employees; build healthy relationships; facilitates learning and results; provides recognition	Gives corrective criticism, negative feedback and negative reinforcement; do not inspire employees to be extraordinary or achieve more than expected; observe employees for mistakes; do not address employees until they are underperforming	Lazy, non-committal and complacent; avoids any involvement and personal interaction with employees; non-responsive to problems; hesitates to take action; delay responses	Dangles the carrot and stick before employees to accomplish goals; negotiate with employees
Focus	People	Self	Self	Self
Productivity Outcome	Achievements	Results	Reduced Productivity	Results
Relationship Outcome	Avoids Loneliness	Likely Experiences Loneliness	Likely Experiences Loneliness	Likely Experiences Loneliness

Transactional leadership, either through management-by-exception, laissez-faire or contingent reward, is the antithesis of coaching-leadership. Transactional leaders extend very little invitation to build relationships with their employees. However, they do create environments of fear and indifference, which is conducive and ripe for loneliness. A new leader's choice of leadership style not only determines their experience with loneliness, but it will also, effectively, govern their ability to get up-to-speed and accomplish organizational objectives through their employees.[13] So it would behoove any leader, who wishes to be successful, both emotionally and organizationally, to lead by coaching and build solid healthy relationships with their employees.

The anatomy of a Work Relationship

Learn Something New

Make it a habit to learn something new about the employee each week. "Knowledge increases confidence."[14] The more you know about your employees, the more capable you will become at anticipating their needs. This may sound strange, but the reality is, managers are responsible for ensuring their staff has what it needs to be productive.[15]

Transparency

Healthy relationships are transparent relationships.[16] It starts with you being honest with yourself about your own knowledge skills and abilities; about what you bring to the table of your department, organization or business.[17] Robb Thompson, pastor of Family Harvest Church says, "The person in your life who is most susceptible to deception is you."[18] He goes on to say, individuals are willing to give others a piece of truth they are not willing to give to themselves.

So managers should know their own limitations and be honest about them. Admit where they need the most help and then allow their employees to help them in the area.

No Judgment

Leaders should resist the urge to pass judgment.[19] It is important they do not rush to judge employees, as their initial perception of the employee's situation is usually not fully accurate. The leader's understanding of a matter is limited because what they know is only what has been revealed to them, which is never the full story.

As leaders begin to look at coaching-leadership and what it takes to be an effective one, they will see the core competencies for this role will require them to know and engage employees from the position of relationship. The relationship starts with building trust and intimacy.[20] Just remember, the deeper the relationships, the deeper the personal influence, the less loneliness experienced.

CONCLUDING REMARKS

We hear all the time from those in leadership positions that being in leadership is lonely. Leadership loneliness is increasingly becoming an epidemic and is negatively affecting leaders in business, in the church and in education. *Leaders Don't Have To Be Lonely*, the goal was to inform new managers that while they may be currently experiencing loneliness, they don't have to live with loneliness forever. There are changes one can make to their leadership routine which will increase their chances of having engaging relationships with their employees. One such remedy for leadership loneliness is the leader's transformation to a coaching-leadership role: a role of trust and intimacy building, through powerful questions, active listening, and direct communications.

A leader who decides to transform himself into a coaching-leader understands he will be building engaging relationships with employees, which will eventually lead to the employee's learning, improved performance and personal growth. The leader also knows becoming a coaching-leader will engender opportunities to build relationships,which will diminish the "us versus them" attitude, creating a friendly environment where employees are willing to speak up and share information.

The bottom line in Leaders Don't Have To Be Lonely is, the more meaningful the engagement, the less likely a leader will have to go through the pain of loneliness. Choosing to lead as a coach means focusing on establishing trust and intimacy with employees, and developing relationships allowing discourse to take place between the manager and employee on a more frequent basis.

However,choosing a coaching-leadership style will mean relinquishing the need to manage as a transactional leader, whose behavior can range from being corrective, critical, negative, to being lazy, non-committal and complacent. As you might imagine, this management style is less likely to endear employees to the leader, and is more likely to cause employees to avoid their leaders at all cost, consequently leading to leadership loneliness.

I hope that having read this book gives you a fresh look at why you may be experiencing loneliness and what you can do to eliminate it in your own life. If you are committed to making the transformation from a transactional leader to a coaching-leader, then make a decision to do something different every day until you are experiencing engaging interaction with employees and the loneliness is no more.

COACHING RESOURCES

Coaching Conversation Agenda

The coaching agenda is the "what" of the coaching conversation. The coaching-leader should use the initial meeting for setting the foundation of the coaching agreement.[1] The coaching-leader can use this initial meeting as a get acquainted session with the employee, but also must use the time to clarify what coaching is, what the employee can expect from the coaching-leader and any logistics the coaching-leader has put in place.

Coaching Conversation Agenda

Initial Coaching Discussion
1. Introductions and backgrounds
2. What employee understands about coaching
3. Clarification of role of coach through coach's eyes
4. In what way the employee might benefit from coaching
5. Employee's feeling about a coaching relationship
6. Logistics and expectations of coaching sessions
7. What specific issues or problems the employee wishes to address

Agenda for Subsequent Coaching Discussions

1.	Business Review
2.	Employee Issues (Problems, Concerns, Opportunities, Challenges)
3.	Action Plan Review
4.	New Actions to be Taken

Just a quick note here: the agenda is a guideline for the points the coaching-leader should cover each session. However, the coaching-leader should be sure to implement the coaching model throughout. Ask questions, allow employees time for reflection, discuss action steps, discuss what they have learned from the completion of previous action steps, and acknowledge accomplished goals.

Performance Discussion Form

Use the Performance Discussion Form to document important information to be captured during the coaching discussion. To ensure both the coaching-leader and the employee have identical information at the end of the discussion, it's advised that the coaching-leader give a copy to the employee and keep a copy for himself. The coaching-leader will use this form to refresh their memory during future discussions.

Performance Discussion Form

As your coaching-leader, I want to help you grow, change, develop, and achieve your performance goals. I will challenge you to live out your values and reach your potential through our focused conversations. And will remain objective in order for you to dialogue with me without fear of reprisal, either formal or informal. Our relationship starts with your agenda, your values, and your initiative. You are responsible for your work assignments, and you will make the choices about what actions to take and what we work on together. I'll provide support, accountability, perspective, and resources for your change goals.

Name: _____

Performance Goals to Work On:_____

_____

_____

_____

Foreseeable Challenges to Goal Completion: _____

_____

_____

_____

Action Steps:

1.

2.

3.

4.

5.

Goals Accomplished:

1.

2.

3.

4.

Organizational Learnings:

_____

_____

_____

_____

Employee Signature:

Coaching-Leader Signature:

Figures

Tables

ENDNOTES

1   John White, *Excellence in Leadership; Reaching Goals with Prayer, Courage & Determination* (Downers Grove, IL: InterVarsity Press, 1986), 10.

2   Ellen Clair Lamb, "How A Manager Becomes a Leader: What Makes the Difference?" *Community Banker* 11, no. 4, (2002): 28-33.

3   Patty Godin, Achieving Vision: Managers vs Leaders. *Manage* 50, no. 1 (Aug 1998): 10-12.

4   Robin M. L. Johnson, *BlackBoard*, January 8, 2012, accessed March 16, 2013, https://regent.blackboard.com/webapps/portal/frameset.jsp?tab_tab_group_id=_2_1&url=%2F-webapps%2Fblackboard%2Fexecute%2Flauncher%3F-type%3DCourse%26id%3D_92929_1%26url%3D.

5   PattyGodin, "Achieving vision: Managers vs. Leaders," *Manage*50, no. 1, (1998): 10-12.

6   Lamb,How A Manager Becomes A Leader.

7   Ibid.

8   Ira Chaleff, *The Courageous Follower: Standing up to and for our leaders* (San Francisco, CA: Berrett-Koehler, 2009), 13-20.

9   Robert Kelly, *The Power of Followership* (New York, NY: A Currency Box, 1992), 41.

10   Peter Northouse, *Leadership: Theory and Practice*, (Thousand Oaks, CA: Sage Publications, Inc, 2007), and John W. Hunt, "Command and Control the Boss: Hierarchies Are Still Strong, So How Can Those with Less Power Learn to Influence Those with More?" *Financial Times* 2001:

11   Carnegie, Dale,*How to Win Friends & Influence People*, (New York, NY: Pocket Books).

12   Manfred F.R. Kets de Vries, "The Leadership Mystique," *Academy of Management Executive* 8, no. 3 (1994): 73-93.

13   Peter Northouse, *Leadership: Theory and Practice*, (Thousand Oaks, CA: Sage Publications, Inc, 2007), 3 and Victor H Vroom and Arthur G Jago, "The Role of the Situation in Leadership," *American Psychologist* (American Psychological Association) 62, no. 1 (January 2007): 17-24.

14   John W. Hunt, "It's Lonely and Tough at the Top: Contrary To Popular Opinion, Chief Executives are often Sad and Isolated Introverts." *Financial Times*, 7, no. 20 (2000): 20.

15   Ira Chaleff, *The Courageous Follower: Standing up to and for our leaders*, (San Francisco, CA: Berrett-Koehler, 2009).

16   The Wall Street Journal, *What Are The Common Mistakes of New Managers?* (n.d.), accessed October 6, 2013, http://guides.wsj.com/management/developing-a-leadership-style/what-are-the-common-mistakes-of-new-managers/.

17   Thomas J. Saporito, *It's Time to Acknowledge CEO Loneliness*, (February 15, 2012), accessed October 6, 2013, http://blogs.hbr.org/2012/02/its-time-to-acknowledge-ceo-lo/.

18   John W. Hunt, "It's Lonely and Tough at the Top: Contrary To Popular Opinion, Chief Executives are often Sad and Isolated Introverts." *Financial Times*, (2000).

19   Kendra Cherry, "Loneliness: Causes, Effects and Treatments for Loneliness," Psychology, (n.d.), accessed June 6, 2013, http://psychology.about.com/od/psychotherapy/a/loneliness.htm.

20   Jenni Catron, "Gifted for Leadership: Women Called into Ministry," Christianity Today, (March 18, 2013), accessed May 29, 2013, http://www.giftedforleadership.com/2013/03/finding_support_in_the_lonely.html.

21   Cacioppo, John T. and William Patrick,*Loneliness: Human Nature and he Need for Social Connection,* (New York City, NY: W.W. Norton & Company, Inc, 2008), 5.

22   Ibid.

23   Robert Dalleck, *Harry S. Truman,* (New York, NY: Time Books, Henry Holt & Company, 2008), 49.

24   Peter Baker, "A President Besieged and Isolated, Yet at Ease," Washington Post, (July 2, 2007), accessed October 6, 2013, http://www.washingtonpost.com/wp-dyn/content/article/2007/07/01/AR2007070101356.html.

25   Donald T. Phillips, *Martin Luther King, Jr. on Leadership*, New York, NY: Warner Books, 1998).

26   Marian N. Ruderman and Patricia J. Ohlott,*The Realities of Management Promotion,* Study, Center for Creative Leadership, Greensboro: Center for Creative Leadership, 1994, 62.

27   Marcus W Dickson, D Brent Smith, Michael W Grojean, and Mark Ehrhart, "An Organizational Climate Regarding Ethics: The Outcome of Leader Values and The Practices that Reflect Them," *The Leadership Quarterly* 12 (2001): 197-217.

28   Catron, Gifted for Leadership.

29   Peter Block, *Community: The Structure of Belonging*, (San Francisco, CA: Berrett-Koehler Publishers, 2009).

30   John Whitmore, *Coaching for Performance: GROWing people, performance and purpsoe*, (Naperville, IL: Nicholas Brealey, 2002), 8

31   J. M. Hunt and J. R. Weintraub, *The Coaching Organization: A Strategy for Developing Leaders*, (Thousand Oaks, CA: Sage Publications, 2007), 7.

Chapter 2

1   Frances J Milliken, Elizabeth W. Morrison, and Patricia F. Hewlin, "An Exploratory Study of Employee Silence: Issues that Employees Don't Communicate Upward and Why," *Journal of Management Studies* 40, no. 6 (August 2003): 1453-76.

2   Taris G Amogbokpa, "The Connection between The Two Facets of Trust (Supervisor Trust and Subordinate Trust) and Leader-Member Exchange Relationship in Two Manufacturing Organizations," Dissertation, School of Business, Capella University, 2010, 127.

3   Steven V Manderscheid and Alexandre Ardichvilli, "A Conceptual Model of Leadership Transition," *Performance Improvement Quarterly* (Wiley InterScience) 20, no. 3/4 (2008): 113-129.

4   M. Heffernan, "Is This Why Employees Don't Tell You Bad News?," *CBS Network News*, May 2011, accessed July 26, 2011, http://www.bnet.com/blog/business-strategy/is-this-why-employees-dont-tell-you-bad-news/1748.

5   Appelbaum, Steven H, John Molson, and Miguel Valero, "The Crucial First Three Months: An Analysis of Leadership Transition Traps and Successes," *Journal of American Academy of Business* 11, no. 1 (March 2007): 1-8.

6   Frances J Milliken and Elizabeth Wolfe Morrison, "Shades of Silence: Emerging Themes and Future Directions for Research on Silence in Organizations," *Journal of Management Studies* 40, no. 6 (September 2003): 1563-1568.

7   Frances Bowen and Kate Blackmon, "Spirals of Silence: The Dynamic Effects of Diversity on Organizational Voice," *Journal of Management Studies* 40, no. 6 (September 2003): 1393-1417.

8   Sonya Fontenot Premeaux and Arthur G Bedeian, "Breaking the Silence: The Moderating Effects of Self-Monitoring in Predicting Speaking Up in the Workplace," *Journal of Management Studies* 40, no. 6 (September 2003): 1537-1562.

9   Bowen and Blackmon, Spirals of Silence.

10   Milliken and Morrison, Shades of Silence.

11   Milliken and Morrison, Shades of Silence.

12   Milliken and Morrison, Shades of Silence.

13   MarieAnn North, "The Isolation Factor," *Healthcare Financial Management* 61, no. 10 (October 2007): 108,110.

14 Appelbaum, Molson and Valero, The Crucial First Three Months.

15 Appelbaum, Molson and Valero, The Crucial First Three Months.

16 Manderscheid and Ardichvilli, A Conceptual Model of Leadership Transition.

17 Appelbaum, Molson, and Valero, "The Crucial First Three Months.

18 "Core Competencies,"International Coach Federation,last modified 2013,accessed September 6, 2013, http://www.coachfederation.org/icfcredentials/core-competencies/.

Chapter 5

1   1 Giles Slade, The Big Disconnect: The Story of Technology and Loneliness. (Amherst, NY: Prometheus Books, 2012), 9.

2   4 Edutopia, The Digital Generation, (n.d.), accessed July 22, 2013, http://www.edutopia.org/digital-generation.

3   Business Wire, "Survey Shows Americans Would Rather Give up Their Televisions, Smartphones and Tablets Than Their Computers," Business Wire, (May 29, 2013), accessed September 1, 2013, http://www.businesswire.com/news/home/20130529005228/en/Survey-Shows-Americans-Give-Televisions-Smartphones-Tablets.

4   Sherry Turkle, Alone Together: Why We Expect More from Technology and Less from Each Other, (New York, NY: Basic Books, 2011), 154.

5   Stephen Marche, "Is Facebook Making Us Lonely?" The Atlantic,April 2, 2012, accessed July 9, 2013 http://www.theatlantic.com/magazine/archive/2012/05/is-facebook-making-us-lonely/308930/.

6   Marche, Is Facebook Making Us Lonely?

7   Slade, The Big Disconnect.

8   Andy Braner, "Lonely Inside the World of Technology," *Huffington Post*, July 05, 2013, accessed July 09, 2013, http://www.huffingtonpost.com/andy-braner/lonely-inside-the-world_b_3551505.html.

9   Glenn Ebersole, "Reading Body Language Is A Strategic Skill In Business Dealings, According To Your Strategic Thinking Business Coach," *Evan Carmichael Business* Coach, (n.d.), accessed July 10, 2013, http://www.evancarmichael.com/Business-Coach/223/Reading-Body-Language-Is-A-Strategic-Skill-In-Business-Dealings-According-To-Your-Strategic-Thinking-Business-Coach.html.

10   Herb Oestreich, "Let's Dump the 55%, 38%, 7% Rule," *BDRP*, (n.d.), accessed September 1, 2013, http://www.bdrp.nl/documenten/mehrabian_oestreich.pdf,and Judith Pearson PhD, "Debunking The 55%, 38%, 7% Rule,"*Hodu*.com, (January 2006), accessed July 12, 2013, http://hodu.com/rule.shtml.

11   Judith Pearson, PhD, "Debunking The 55%, 38%, 7% Rule "January 2006, accessed July 12, 2013, http://hodu.com/rule.shtml.

12   Anthony K Tjan, "Don't Send That Email, Pick Up The Phone," *HBR Blog Network*, (November 1, 2011), accessed

July 10, 2013, http://blogs.hbr.org/tjan/2011/11/dont-send-that-email-pick-up-t.html.

13   Chantal Besson, Daria Graf, Insa Hartung, Barbara Kropf-hausser, and Severine Voisard, "The Importanceof Non-Verbal Communication in Professional Interpretation," Paper, University of Geneva, 2004.

14   Beth Greenwood, "The Positive Effects of Face-to-Face Communication in the Workplace," *Chron*, (n.d.), accessed September 1, 2013, http://work.chron.com/positive-effects-facetoface-communication-workplace-3561.html.

15   Max Wideman, *Positive Body Language*, (April 2002), accessed July 11, 2013, http://www.maxwideman.com/issacons4/iac1435/sld001.htm.

16   Max Wideman, "Negative Body Language," (April 2002), accessed July 11, 2013, http://maxwideman.com/issacons4/iac1436/sld001.htm.

17   Mind Tools, "Body Language," *Mind Tools*, (n.d.), accessed July 2, 2013, http://www.mindtools.com/pages/article/Body_Language.htm.

18   "Core Competencies,"International Coach Federation,last modified 2013,accessed September 6, 2013, http://www.coachfederation.org/icfcredentials/core-competencies/.

19   Kirsten Weir, "The Pain of Social Rejection," *American Pyschological Association*, (April 2012), accessed July 12, 2013, http://www.apa.org/monitor/2012/04/rejection.aspx

20   Ibid.

21   Ibid.

22   C. Nathan DeWall, and Brad J. Bushman. "Social Acceptance and Rejection: The Sweet and the Bitter," *Current Directions in Psychological Science* 20, no. 4 (2011): 256-260.

23   F. Scott Addis, "Using Rejection As A Motivator," *Unpublished Notes,* (n.d.): 98-100.

24   Sherry Turkle, "We Would Rather Text than Talk," *The Economic Times,* (July 9, 2011), accessed October 6, 2013, http://0search. proquest.com.library.regent.edu/docview/875561279?accountid=13479.

25   Sherry Turkle, "The Flight from Conversation," *Sunday Review,* (April 21, 2012), accessed July 20, 2013, http://www.nytimes. com/2012/04/22/opinion/sunday/the-flight-from-conversation.html?pagewanted=all&_r=0.

26   Weir, The Pain of Social Rejection and Marche, Is Facebook Making Us Lonely?

27   Lowell Gaertner, Jonathan Iuzzini, and Erin M O'Mara, "When Rejection by One Fosters Aggression against Many: Multiple-victim aggression as a consequence of social rejection and perceived groupness," *Journal of Experimental Social Psychology* 44 (2008): 958-970.

28   John T.Cacioppo and William Patrick, *Loneliness: Human Nature and he Need for Social Connection,* (New York City, NY: W.W. Norton & Company, Inc, 2008): 18.

29   J. M. Kouzes and B. Z. Posner, *The Leadership Challenge* (San Francisco, CA: Jossey-Boss, Inc., 2007), 21.

30   Department of Research, "School Shootings," (December 2012), accessed August 26, 2013 http://holology.com/shooting.html# 9.

31   Biswajit Das and Jyoti Shankar Sahoo, "Social Networking Sites - A Critical Analysis of Its Impact on Personal and Social Life," *International Journal of Business and Social Science* 2, no. 14 (August 2011): 222-228

32   International Coach Federation, Core Competencies.

33   Blaine Donais, "Training Managers in Handling Conflict," *Canadian HR Reporter*, March 12, 2007: 13,17.

34   A. R. Elangovan, "Managerial Interventon in Organizational Disputes: Testing A Prescriptive Model of Strategy Selection," *The International Journal of Conflict Management* 9, no. 4 (October 1998): 301-335.

35   Daniel Goleman, "Managing Conflict," *Leadership Excellence* 30, no. 3 (March 2013): 18.

36   A R Elangovan, "Managerial Interventon in Organizational Disputes: Testing A Prescriptive Model of Strategy Selection," *The International Journal of Conflict Management* 9, no. 4 (October 1998): 301-335.

37   . K. A. Jehn, "A Qualitative analysis of Conflict Types and Dimensions in Organizational Groups," *Administrative Science Quarterly* 42, no. 2 (1997): 256-82.

38   Turkle, Flight from Conversation.

39   Greg MacSweeny, "Managing Millenials," *Wall Street & Technology* 30, no. 2 (June 2012).

40   Turkle, The Flight from Conversation.

41   Tjan, Don't Send That Email, Pick Up The Phone.

42   Tjan, Don't Send That Email, Pick Up the Phone.

43   David F Swink, "Managing Conflicts with Email: Why It's So Tempting," *Psychology Today*, January 14, 2010.

44   Reputation.com, "Why Starting A Social Media Fight Could KO Your Online Reputation," *Reputation.com*, (n.d.), accessed July 23, 2013, http://www.reputation.com/reputationwatch/articles/why-starting-social-media-fight-could-ko-your-online-reputation.

45   Tjan, Don't Send That Email, Pick Up The Phone.

46   Sades, The Big Disconnect.

47   Daniel Goleman, "Managing Conflict," *Leadership Excellence* 30, no. 3 (March 2013): 18.

Chapter 4

1   C. Eric Mount, Jr, "American Individualism Reconsidered," *Review of Religious Research*, 22, no. 4 (June 1981): 362-375.

2   Stephen Marche, "Is Facebook Making Us Lonely?" The Atlantic,April 2, 2012, accessed July 9, 2013 http://www.theatlantic.com/magazine/archive/2012/05/is-facebook-making-us-lonely/308930/.

3   Marieke de Mooij and Geert Hofstede, "The Hofstede Model: Applications To Global Branding and Advertising Strategy and Research," *International Journal of Advertising* (Warc) 29, no. 1 (2010): 85-110.

4   Greg Scott, Joseph Ciarrockhi, and Frank P. Deane, "Disadvantages of Being An Individualist in An Individualist Culture: Idiocentrism, Emotional Competence, Stress and Mental Health," *Australian Psychologist* 39, no. 2 (May 2004): 143-153.

5   IOR Global Services, ed., "Cultural Insights: United States," n.d., IOR, accessed July 1, 2013, http://www.iorworld.com/ usa-cultural-insights---worldview---cultural-assumptions--- communication-style---business-practices-pages-485.php.

6   C. Eric Mount, Jr, "American Individualism Reconsidered," *Review of Religious Research*, 22, no. 4 (June 1981): 362-375.

7   Scott and Deane, Disadvantages of Being An Individualist in An Individualist Culture: Idiocentrism, Emotional Competence, Stress and Mental Health.

8   Scott and Deane, Disadvantages of Being An Individualist in An Individualist Culture: Idiocentrism, Emotional Competence, Stress and Mental Health.

9   Ardyth A Norem-Hebeisen and David W Johnson, "The Relationship between Cooperative, Competitive, and Individualistic Attitudes and Differentiated Aspects of Self-Esteem," *Journal of Personality* 49, no. 4 (December 1981): 415-426.

10   Ibid.

11   Ron Ashkenas, Dave Ulrich, Todd Jick, and Steve Kerr, *The Boundaryless Organization: Breaking The Chains of Organizational Structure*, San Francisco, CA: Jossey-Bass, 2002.

12   Éve Laurier, "Razing silos and slabs," *CA Magazine*. (May 2011), accessed August 27, 2011, http:/www.camagazine.

com /archives/print-edition/2011/may/regulars/camagazine49097.aspx.

13 Laurier, Razing silos and slabs.

14 Éve Laurier, "Razing silos and slabs," *CA Magazine*. (May 2011), accessed August 27, 2011, http:/www.camagazine. com /archives/print-edition/2011/may/regulars/camagazine49097.aspx.

15 Gareth Morgan, *Imaginization*. (Newbury Park, CA: Sage Publications, 1993), 83.

16 de Mooij and Hofstede, The Hofstede Model: Applications To Global Branding and Advertising Strategy and Research.

17 Julian Rappaport and Edward Seidman, *Handbook of Community Psychology*. New York, NY: Plenum Publishers, 2000, 68.

18 Steven D Papamarcos, Craig Latshaw, and George W Watson, "Individualism-Collectivism and Incentive System Design as Predictive of Productivity in a Simulated Cellular Manufacturing Environment," *International Journal of Cross Cultural Management* 7, no. 2 (2007): 253-265.

19 Jaymi McCann, "American Boss Released from Chinese Factory Where He Was Held Hostage by Workers for SIX Days," *MailOnline News*, June 27, 2013, accessed June 27, 2013, http:// www.dailymail.co.uk/news/article-2349521/Chip-Starnes-US-boss-released-Chinese-factory-held-hostage.html?ito=-feeds-videoxml.

20 Today Show, "Behind The Wall on NBCNEWS.com," (June 27, 2013), accessed June 27, 2013, http://behindthewall.nbcnews.com/.

21   Colette L. Meehan, "Flat Vs. Hierarchical Organizational Structure," Chron, July 24, 2013, accessed March 14, 2013, http://smallbusiness.chron.com/flat-vs-hierarchical-organizational-structure-724.html.

22   Laurier, Razing silos and slabs.

23   A H Maslow, "A Theory of Human Motivation," *Psychological Review* 50, no. 4 (July 1943): 370-396.

24   Norem-Hebeisen and Johnson, The Relationship between Cooperative, Competitive, and Individualistic Attitudes and Differentiated Aspects of Self-Esteem.

25   Norem-Hebeisen and Johnson, The Relationship between Cooperative, Competitive, and Individualistic Attitudes and Differentiated Aspects of Self-Esteem.

26   collaboration. Dictionary.com. *Collins English Dictionary - Complete & Unabridged 10th Edition.* HarperCollins Publishers, accessed October 10, 2013, http://dictionary.reference.com/browse/collaboration

27   Robin M L Johnson, "Getting Employees to Collaborate Cross-Functionally Amid Inter-Department Culture Differences," Chicago, IL: N/A, (November 2011), 1-4.

28   Ashkenas, Ulrich, Jick, and Kerr, The Boundaryless Organization: Breaking The Chains of Organizational Structure.

29   Ashkenas, Ulrich, Jick, and Kerr, The Boundaryless Organization: Breaking The Chains of Organizational Structure, 40.

Chapter 3

1   "Core Competencies,"International Coach Federation,last modified 2013,accessed September 6, 2013, http://www.coachfederation.org/icfcredentials/core-competencies/.

2   John Whitmore, *Coaching for Performance: GROWing people, performance and purpose,*(Naperville, IL: Nicholas Brealey, 2002), 8.

3   Ibid.

4   Ibid.

5   H Morgan, P Harkins, and M Goldsmith, eds.,*The Art and Practice of Leadership Coaching,*(Hoboken, NJ: John Wiley & Sons, Inc., 2005), 25.

6   Larry Barker, PhD and Kittie Watson, PhD. *Listen* Up, (New York, NY: St. Martin's Griffin, 2000), 13.

7   T G Crane, *The Heart of Coaching: Using Transformational Coaching to Create A High-Performance Culture*, San Diego, CA: FTA Press, 2001, 105.

8   Crane, *The Heart of Coaching*, 38.

9   Vidal-Salazar, Maria Dolores, Vera Ferron-Vilchez, and Eulogio Cordon-Pozo, "Coaching: An Effective Practice for Business Competitiveness," *Competitiveness Review: An International Business Journal* 22, no. 5 (2012): 423-433.

10   Jeffrey Magee, PhD and Jay Kent-Ferraro, PhD, *Coaching for Impact*. Dallas, TX: Brown Books, Inc., 2000.

11   Tony Stoltzfus, *Leadership Coaching: The Disciplines, Skills and Heart of a Christian Coach,*(Virginia Beach, VA: Tony Stoltzfus, 2005), 67.

12   International Coach Federation n.d., Core Competencies.

13   International Coach Federation n.d., Core Competencies.

14   Morgan, Harkins, and Goldsmith, The Art and Practice of Leadership Coaching

15   J. M.Hunt and J. R. Weintraub,*The Coaching Organization: A Strategy for Developing Leaders*,(Thousand Oaks, CA: Sage Publications, 2007),7.

16   Crane, The Heart of Coaching, 31.

17   Jeff Schmitt,"12 Ways to Be the Leader Everyone Wants to Work for,"*Forbes*.com, February 19, 2013, accessed July 29, 2013 http://www.forbes.com/sites/jeffschmitt/2013/02/19/12-ways-to-be-the-leader-everyone-wants-to-work-for/.

18   Kay Greasley, Alan Bryman, Adrew Dainty, Andrew Price, Nicola Naismith, and Robby Soetanto, "Understanding Empowerment from an Employee Perspective," *Team Performance Management* (Emerald Group Publishing) 14, no. 1/2 (2008): 39-55.

19   Ferdinand F Fournies, *Coaching for Improved Work Performance*. New York, NY: McGraw-Hill, 2000.

20   Susan Wright Ed.D, "The Leadership Coach: Creating High Performance in Change," *Banff Centre*, n.d., Accessed July 5, 2013, http://www.banffcentre.ca/leadership/library/pdf/coach_22-24.pdf.

21   J M Hunt and J R Weintraub. *The Coaching Organization: A Strategy for Developing Leaders*, Thousand Oaks, CA: Sage Publications, 2007, 16.

22   Hunt and Weintraub, The Coaching Organization,7.

Chapter 6

1. David B Peterson, PhD and Mary Dee Hicks PhD, *Leader As Coach: Strategies for Coaching and Developing Others*, Minneapolis, MN: Personnel Decisions International, 1996, 28.

2. W. Bradford Swift, DVM, "Are You A Coachable Team Player?"(FirstLine), 9, no. 9 (2013): 26-28.

3. J M Hunt and J R Weintraub, *The Coaching Organization: A Strategy for Developing Leaders*, Thousand Oaks, CA: Sage Publications, 2007, 90.

4. Hunt and Weintraub, The Coaching Organization, 36.

5. "Core Competencies,"International Coach Federation,last modified 2013,accessed September 6, 2013, http://www.coachfederation.org/icfcredentials/core-competencies/.

6. Association of Coaching, "AC Code of Ethics and Good Practice,"*Association for* Coaching, accessed October 28, 2013. http://www.associationforcoaching.com/pages/about/code-ethics-good-practice.

7. International Coach Federation n.d., Core Competencies.

8. Ferdinand F Fournies, *Coaching for Improved Work Performance*. New York, NY: McGraw-Hill, 2000.

9. Hunt and Weintraub, The Coaching Organization, 181.

10. Mary Catherine Moran, "Differentiated Literacy Coaching," *ASCD*. (December 2007), accessed October 6, 2013, http://www.ascd.org/publications/books/107053/chapters/The-Context-for-a-Literacy-Coaching-Continuum.aspx, chapter 1

11. T G Crane, *The Heart of Coaching: Using Transformational Coaching to Create A High-Performance Culture*, San Diego, CA: FTA Press, 2001, 31.

12. John Whitmore, *Coaching for Performance: GROWing people, performance and purpsoe.* Naperville, IL: Nicholas Brealey, 2002 and J M Hunt and J R Weintraub, *The Coaching Organization: A Strategy for Developing Leaders*, Thousand Oaks, CA: Sage Publications, 2007

13. Tony Stoltzfus,*Leadership Coaching: The Disciplines, Skills and Heart of a Christian Coach,* (Virginia Beach, VA: Tony Stoltzfus, 2005), 177.

14. Stoltzfus, Leadership Coaching, 81.

15. M.Goldberg, "Asking The Right Questions As A Coach," *International Coach Federation,* (n.d.),accessed January 10, 2013, http://www.coachfederation.org/includes/docs/003AskingtheRightQuestionsasaCoachGoldbergManchest.pdf.

16. Whitmore 2002, Coaching for Performance, 44.

17. Stan Kontos, *Life at The Next Level: A Step-By-Step Approach to Creating a Life of Personal and Professional Success.* Bloomington, IN: Balboa Press, 2012, 12.

18. Susan Scott, *Fierce Conversations: achieving success at work & in life, one conversation at a time.*(New York, NY: Berkley Books, 2002), 26.

19. Training Zone, "Challenging Coaching Questions," *Training Zone*, (September 13, 2013), accessed October 6, 2013, http://www.trainingzone.co.uk/blogs-post/challenging-coaching-questions/185341.

20. Robert L Dilworth, "Creating Opportunities for Reflection in Action Learning: Nine Important Avenues," *ITAP International*, (2013), accessed September 12, 2013, http://www.itapintl.com/facultyandresources/articlelibrarymain/creating-opportunities-for-reflection-in-action-learning-nine-important-avenues.html.

21. Joseph A Raelin, "I Don't Have Time to Think! versus the Art of Reflective Practice," *Reflections*, 2002: 66-80.

22. Ibid.

23. Linda Finlay, "Reflecting on Reflective Practice," *PBPL Practice-based Professional Learning Centre*, The Open University, n.d., accessed on September 2, 2013, *http://www.open.ac.uk/cetl-workspace/cetlcontent/documents/4bf2b48887459.pdf.*

24. Raelin, I Don't Have Time To Think!

25. Raelin, "I Don't Have Time to Think!

26. Jeff Patmore, Tanya Goldhaber, and Ben Hardy, "Understanding the Power of Reflection," Research Paper, Cambridge, 2011, 1-4.

27. Raelin, I Don't Have Time To Think!

28. Jack Mezirow, "Fostering Critical Reflection in Adulthood: A Guide to Transformative and Emancipatory Learning," *Lingnan University*, (2011), accessed September 15, 2013, http://www.ln.edu.hk/osl/conference2011/output/breakout/4.4%20%5Bref%5DHow%20Critical%20Reflection%20triggers%20Transformative%20Learning%20-%20Mezirow.pdf.

29. Robert L. Dilworth, "Creating Opportunities for Reflection in

Action Learning: Nine Important Avenues," *ITAP International,* n.d., accessed September 12, 2013, http://www.itapintl.com/facultyandresources/articlelibrarymain/creating-opportunities-for-reflection-in-action-learning-nine-important-avenues.html.

30. Goodstone Group, "Our Approach,"*Goodstone*, (n.d.), accessed October 6, 2013, http://goodstonegroup.com/our-approach/elements-of-a-typical-goodstone-coaching-engagement/.

31. Erik de Haan, "Back To Basics II: How The Research on Attachment and Reflective-Self Function is Relevant for Coaches and Consultants Today," *International Coaching Psychology Review* 7, no. 2 (2012): 194-209.

32. Jeffrey M. Hiatt, *ADKAR: A Model for Change in Business, Government and Our* Community, (Loveland, CO: Prosci Research, 2006), 2.

33. University of Wisconsin-Milwaukee, "Resistance to Change," *University of Wisconsin-Milwaukeee*, (n.d.), accessed October 6, 2013, http://www4.uwm.edu/cuts/bench/change.htm.

34. Mark Goulston, "Practical Tips for Overcoming Resistance," *HBR Blog Network*, (July 1, 2013), accessed October 7, 2013, http://blogs.hbr.org/2013/07/practical-tips-for-overcoming-r/

35. Ibid.

36. Ibid.

37. Ron Ashkenas, Dave Ulrich, Todd Jick, and Steve Kerr. *The Boundaryless Organization: Breaking The Chains of Organizational Structure*, (San Francisco, CA: Jossey-Bass, 2002), 40.

38. Steven V Manderscheid and Alexandre Ardichvilli, "A Conceptual Model of Leadership Transition," *Performance Improvement Quarterly* (Wiley InterScience) 20, no. 3/4 (2008): 113-129.

39. Linda Ackerman-Anderson, "Getting Smart About Employee Resistance to Change," *Change Leaders Network*, (n.d.), accessed October 6, 2013, http://changeleadersnetwork.com/free-resources/getting-smart-about-employee-resistance-to-change-part-one.

40. Jeffrey D Ford and Laurie W. Ford, "Decoding Resistance to Change," *Harvard Business Review*, (April 2009), accessed October 6, 2013, http://hbr.org/2009/04/decoding-resistance-to-change/ar/1.

41. Whitmore, Coaching for Performance, 97.

42. Whitmore, Coaching for Performance, 84.

43. Whitmore, Coaching for Performance, 80.

44. Yossi Ives and Elaine Cox, *Goal-Focused Coaching: Theory and Practice,* New York, NY: Routledge, 2012, 62.

45. Whitmore, Coaching for Performance, 89-90.

46. Stoltzfus, Leadership Coaching.

47. Todd E Conklin, *Simple Revolutionary Acts: Ideas to Revitalize Yourself and Your Workplace*, Lincoln, NE: IUniverse, 2004, Section.3

48. J M Kouzes and B Z Posner, *The Leadership Challenge,* San Francisco, CA: Jossey-Boss, Inc., 1995, ch9.

49. Ashgate, "Defining Action Learning: What Is It and What Is It for?" *Ashgate*, n.d., accessed September 14, 2013, http://www.ashgate.com/pdf/SamplePages/actlearnch1.pdf.

50. Don Clark, "Active Learning Defined,"*NWLink*, (May 12, 2009), accessed October 6, 2013, http://www.nwlink.com/~donclark/hrd/learning/active.html.

51. University of Virginia, "A Framework for Thinking about Feedback and Evaluation & Learning,"*University of Virginia*, (February 28, 2005), accessed October 6, 2013,

52. http://faculty.virginia.edu/orgsthatlearn/CoursePortfolio/051-Framework-For-Thinking-About-Evaluation.pdf.

53. Michael J Marquardt, "Action Learning"*By George*, (February 18, 2004), accessed October 6, 2013, http://www.gwu.edu/~bygeorge/021804/actionlearning.html.

54. Jonathan Passmore, *Psychometric in coaching: using psychological and psychometric tools for development*, London: Kogan Page Limited, 2008, chapter 2.

55. Ferdinand F Fournies, *Coaching for Improved Work Performance*. New York, NY: McGraw-Hill, 2000, 178.

56. Ibid.

57. "Core Competencies,"International Coach Federation,last modified 2013,accessed September 6, 2013, http://www.coachfederation.org/icfcredentials/core-competencies/.

58. J M Hunt and J R Weintraub. *The Coaching Organization: A Strategy for Developing Leaders*, Thousand Oaks, CA: Sage Publications, 2007, 184

59. International Coach Federation, Core Competencies.

60. Hunt and Weintraub, The Coaching Organization, 184.

61. International Coaching Federation, Core Competencies.

62. Hunt and Weintraub 2007, The Coaching Organization, 187.

Chapter 7

1. Sarah Rubenstein, "When a Co-Worker Becomes The Boss: Can Friendship Last?" *Wall Street Journal*,(May 24, 2005), accessed October 6, 2013, http://online.wsj.com/article/SB111599157991232943.html.

2. Merrill C Anderson, PhD, Candice Frankovelgia, PsyD, and Gina Hernez-Broome, PhD, "Creating Coaching Cultures: What Business Leaders Expect and Strategies to Get There," *A CCL Research White Paper*, Center for Creative Leadership and Cylient, (n.d.).

3. Steven V Manderscheid and Alexandre Ardichvilli, "A Conceptual Model of Leadership Transition," *Performance Improvement Quarterly* (Wiley InterScience) 20, no. 3/4 (2008): 113-129.

4. Ibid.

5. Ibid.

6. Robert J Spinelli, "Tranformational, Transactional and Laissez-Faire Leadership: An Investigation of Bass's (1985) Theory In the Hospital Administrative Environment," Dissertation, H. Wayne Huizenga School of Business and Entrepreneurship, Nova Southeastern University, 2004, 34-35.

7. Peter Northouse, *Leadership: Theory and Practice*, (Thousand Oaks, CA: Sage Publications, Inc, 2007), 3 and Victor H Vroom and Arthur G Jago, "The Role of the Situation in Leadership," *Amer-*

ican Psychologist (American Psychological Association) 62, no. 1 (January 2007): 185.

8. Ibid.

9. J C Sarros and J. C. Santora, "The Transformational-Transactional Leadership Model in Practice," *Leadership & Organization Development Journal* 22, no. 8 (2001): 383-393.

10. Ibid.

11. Ibid.

12. Northouse 2007, Leadership, 185.

13. Manderscheid and Ardichvilli, A Conceptual Model of Leadership Transition.

14. Mike Murdock, *Seeds of Wisdom*, Vol. 2. TX, Ft Worth, (n.d.).

15. Ruth Mayhew, "How to Meet Employee Needs in an Organization," *Chron*, (n.d.), accessed October 15, 2013, http://work. chron.com/meet-employee-needs-organization-9244.html.

16. Peter G Vajda, "Why Being Transparent Can be Challenging," *True North Partnering*, (2012).

17. Robb D Thompson, *The 10 Critical Laws of Relationship*. Tinley Park, IL: Family Harvest Church, (2005).

18. Ibid.

19. Murdock, Seeds of Wisdom.

20. Core Competencies," International Coach Federation, last modified 2013, accessed September 6, 2013, http://www.coachfederation.org/icfcredentials/core-competencies/.

Appendix

1. Core Competencies, International Coach Federation, last modified 2013, accessed September 6, 2013, http://www.coachfederation.org/icfcredentials/core-competencies/.

·

CPSIA information can be obtained
at www.ICGtesting.com
Printed in the USA
FFHW012209100619
52921154-58517FF